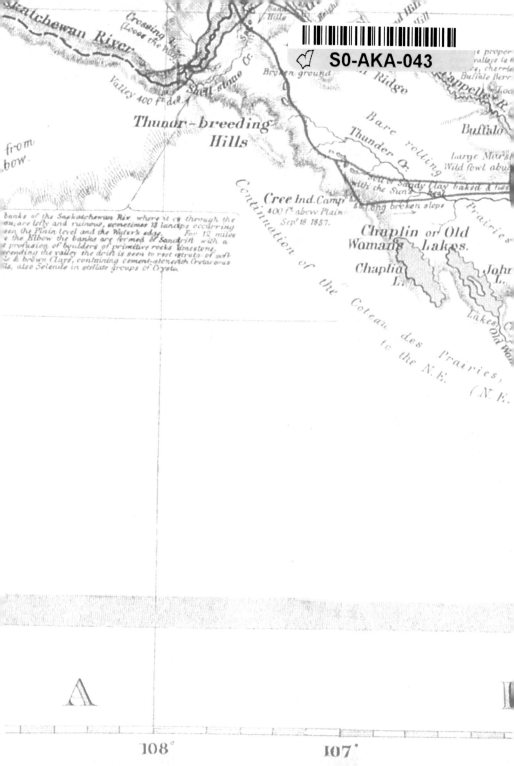

…tchewan River

Crossing
(loses the way)

Valley 400 ft.dp

Shell stone &

Sandy
Hills

Height

Broken ground

al Hill

e proper
valleys is
o, cherries
Buffalo Berr

Ridge

appelle R.

Thunder-breeding
Hills

Bare rolling

Thunder Cr.

with the Sun's

Buffalo

large Marsh
Wild fowl abu

Sandy Clay baked & bes

from
bow.

Cree Ind. Camp
400 ft. above Plain
Sep.t 18 1857.

Continuation

of

the

long broken slope

Chaplin or Old
Woman's Lakes.

Prairies

banks of the Saskatchewan Riv. where it cu through the
an, are lofty and ruinous, sometimes 13 landps occurring
een the Plain level and the Water's edge. For 12 miles
e the Elbow the banks are formed of Sandrift with a
t profusion of boulders of primitive rocks limestone,
scending the valley the drift is seen to rest estrata of soft
e & brown Clays, containing cement-stone with Cretaceous
ls, also Selenite in stellate groups of Crysta.

Coteau

Chaplin
L.

John
L.

Lakes

des

Prairies,

to

the

N.E.

Old Wo

(N.E.

A

108°

107°

BOOKS BY SHARON BUTALA

Country of the Heart
Queen of the Headaches
The Gates of the Sun
Luna
Fever
Upstream
The Fourth Archangel
The Perfection of the Morning
Coyote's Morning Cry
The Garden of Eden

WILD STONE HEART

Sharon Butala

WILD STONE HEART

An Apprentice in the Fields

Harper*Flamingo*Canada
A Phyllis Bruce Book

Wild Stone Heart:
An Apprentice in the Fields
Copyright © 2000 by Sharon Butala.
All rights reserved. No part of this book may
be used or reproduced in any manner
whatsoever without prior written permission
except in the case of brief quotations embodied
in reviews. For information address
HarperCollins Publishers Ltd,
55 Avenue Road, Suite 2900,
Toronto, Ontario,
Canada M5R 3L2.

www.harpercanada.com

HarperCollins books may be purchased for
educational, business, or sales promotional use.
For information please write:
Special Markets Department,
HarperCollins Canada,
55 Avenue Road, Suite 2900,
Toronto, Ontario,
Canada M5R 3L2.

First HarperFlamingo ed.
ISBN 0-00-255397-X
First HarperPerennialCanada ed.
ISBN 0-00-639129-X

The author wishes to thank the Canada Council
for financial assistance with this work.

Reprinted with the permission of
Simon & Schuster, from *Walking in the Sacred
Manner: Healers, Dreamers, and Pipe Carriers –
Medicine Women of the Plains Indians* by Mark
St. Pierre and Tilda Long Soldier. Originally told
to Mark St. Pierre by Colleen Cutshall.
Copyright © 1995 by Mark St. Pierre
and Tilda Long Soldier

Endpaper map courtesy of Aquila Books, Calgary
www.aquilabooks.com

Canadian Cataloguing in Publication Data

Butala, Sharon, 1940–
Wild stone heart : an apprentice in the fields

"A Phyllis Bruce book".
ISBN 0-00-255397-X

1. Butala, Sharon, 1940– —Homes
and haunts—Saskatchewan.
2. Landscape—Saskatchewan.
I. Title.

PS8553.U6967Z53 2000   C818'.54
C00-931210-2
PR9199.3.B798Z478 2000

00 01 02 03 04 HC 5 4 3 2 1
Printed and bound in the United States

CONTENTS

To
The Spirits of the Field

Iyan, the rock, existed in a void; it was dark and lonely there. Iyan wished to create something other, so that he would not be lonely and so that he could have some power over something other than himself. He pierced himself, and his blood, which was blue, flowed out until he was shriveled, hard and powerless. What came from him formed *Maka Ina* [Mother Earth]. The blue also formed the oceans, but the released powers could not reside in the water, so they formed the blue sky dome and called it *Mahpiyato* [blue sky].

The energy given up by the rock, now hard and powerless, is *Taku Skan Skan*, that which moves all things. This power was now diffused into the female earth, the male sky, and the waters.

— From a Lakota Creation Story, as told by Colleen Cutshall in *Walking in the Sacred Manner*, Mark St. Pierre and Tilda Long Soldier

WILD STONE HEART

Prologue

HAUNTINGS

OUR HOUSE WAS HAUNTED. IT WAS HAUNTED FROM THE time it was an unfinished shell sitting on its foundation next door to the small log house in which we lived in a wide river valley some miles from Eastend, Saskatchewan (so-called because it's at the east end of the Cypress Hills), until recently, a period of a good twenty years. I say "haunted" blithely, without apprehension, not caring any more if I'm believed or not. I know no other word for what happened to us and there is no other explanation, although for a very long time I would never have said so out loud.

Since 1913, when my husband's father had arrived from Slovakia to join his two brothers already in Canada, the Butalas had slowly built up their ranch on the wide grasslands of the northern Great Plains, just over the border from Montana, and in the extreme southwest corner of Saskatchewan. By the time Peter and I married in 1976, it was more than thirteen thousand acres. Here Peter and his siblings had been raised, and here I came as a bride, but as the ranch was forty dirt-or-gravel, often impassable miles from the small hay farm the Butalas also owned, we'd decided, after much argument, to locate our new house at the farm. This decision was based on the long distance the ranch was from the nearest town, on the inadequate roads which were often blocked in winter, and especially on the ranch's openness to the elements. There was not a tree or any other barrier to break the sweep of winter blizzards which struck the cattle, horses, and buildings with overwhelming, barely endurable force.

The haunting of our new house began the summer of 1979 when it first arrived in the hay farm's yard. By "yard" I mean the five or so fenced acres separating the open fields from the corrals, vegetable garden, and the buildings: the small barn that could stable a half-dozen horses or a few sick cows and their calves; two Quonsets, one for machinery storage and one shelter for the calves in winter; a chickenshed; a few ramshackle wooden granaries now used to store old tires, broken furniture, or out-of-date tools—rusted, once three-pronged pitchforks the bundle-pitchers on threshing crews used, cracked and split leather harnesses for teams, leaky wooden butter churns, defunct wringer-washers, and so on. There were also a couple of small, old frame buildings—empty now and defying naming but which might once have been the first shacks of settlers—and the deteriorating old log house in which we were currently living.

Provincial Archives documents had shown us that the yard was inhabited as early as 1912, but the Butalas hadn't purchased the place until 1949, when they decided they needed to be able to grow their own winter feed for their cattle herd, as the ranch was too arid to produce enough itself. They also wanted the hay farm because, located as it was in a wide and fairly deep river valley, it could provide shelter for the cattle during the worst months of the winter.

The house was a modest, typically prairie, three-bedroom bunga-low with a bath and a half, a "ready-to-move," framed and nearly finished in a city for the purpose of being moved to a rural lot, a solu-tion to the problem of finding contractors willing to work on remote farms and ranches like ours. We set it in a protective bend of our little river, the Frenchman, a shallow, muddy body of water full of perch, jackfish, carp, muskrat, and beaver about forty miles south of the Cypress Hills. At this point it is perhaps fifty feet wide and, having started in the Cypress Hills, runs on a hundred miles east through the driest of the dry area (called the "Palliser Triangle" after John Palliser, who in the 1850s had delineated its boundaries, reporting it to the British as unsuitable for agriculture), and then south over the Canadian-American border until it finally ends in the Missouri–Mississippi river system. The border is the "Medicine Line" of the Amerindians of the Plains. The term is probably more accurately translatable as a potent spirit or power line, since the Amerindian people knew no political borders of the sort the Europeans established and, until the arrival in the late nineteenth century of the first settlers, had roamed freely within their traditional territories wherever the seasons, the supply of grass, and the buffalo took them.

In fact, from its settlement early in this century until the fifties or so, because of its vast, wide-open grassland, southwest Saskatchewan had been largely ranchland which, given the virtual extinction of the plains bison in the 1880s, had hardly been grazed. It must have looked like heaven to ranchers from Montana and farther south whose own rangeland was already beginning to be depleted. But not long after the area was opened to settlers, families started to turn to farming, and the balance was now shifting from one of more ranches than farms to one of more farms than ranches. I was to be the beneficiary of the Butalas' stubborn adherence to the old way of life on the Plains, and it was quite a while before I began to understand that not many families lived as we did, that is, in the midst of many never-ploughed fields—fields still in their natural condition of native grass.

The summer our new house was moved into the yard, my nephew was visiting my teenage son, and since the log house in which Peter, the hired man, and I lived was far too small to hold the boys too and the weather was hot and dry, we set up beds for them in an empty bedroom in the as-yet-unfinished new house, a better solution to the space problem than a tent. But, it soon turned out, the new house was so full of various weird and unexplained noises—or perhaps even more than that, something hovering in the air which caused the boys to glance over their shoulders as they dressed and undressed, to pull the blankets over their heads once the light was out—that one wouldn't sleep there unless the other one was there too.

To tell the truth, I heard those noises when I was working in the house during the day, painting the walls and the ceilings, room by room, but I chose to tell myself that I was imagining them or, when in all sanity I could not pretend they hadn't occurred, that there would be a rational explanation for them if I could be bothered to search for it. But with the housework and the cooking, my work as a rancher's wife—chasing cows on horseback, truck-driving, opening and shutting corral gates as cattle were being sorted—and now the painting of the new house, I was working too hard and was far too tired to worry much about anything not immediate and practical. I remember reasoning that since the house had just been moved, it was to be expected that there would be a lot of "settling" as it established itself on its foundation. But mostly I just dismissed the sounds without really allowing myself to think about them. I was so busy that by the time fall had arrived, merely to turn the wheel for a curve in the road on the way into town seemed more than I could manage, and a visit to the doctor revealed that I had become anaemic.

While not without constant tribulation—the plumbers who, after we had waited for weeks, came from seventy-five miles away having left half their equipment behind, had coffee, then went back; various workmen who didn't show up day after day after day while we waited nervously, thinking of another winter in the too small, mice-ridden, and bathroomless log house—by mid-December we'd finished the interior painting, the installation of the kitchen cupboards, the rugs, the vinyl flooring in the kitchen and bathrooms, and the light fixtures, and had connected all the plumbing and electricity. At last, at Christmas, with relief on Peter's part and something close to joy on mine, we moved into the house.

My widowed mother and a younger sister, her husband, and family came from the city to help us celebrate. In order to cook and serve the dinner, we had to keep running back to the log house to bring over dishes and utensils that hadn't been moved yet, and the still curtainless house with its too little furniture—I intended to buy some new pieces in January—echoed noisily with our voices and footsteps. None of that disturbed our good cheer, and in all the excitement and then the distractions of settling into our new home, it was a while before we could no longer hide from ourselves that our beautiful, much-longed-for house had some peculiar goings-on in it.

For a long time we didn't say out loud to anybody, not even to each other—as if not saying it out loud would keep it from being true—that our house was haunted. After all, neither of us entirely believed in ghosts. The happenings that were disturbing us seemed mostly to be on the periphery of our attention. We rarely heard a strange noise directly, but instead became aware of it an instant after it had happened so that we were never sure it really had. We were constantly asking each other, *What was that?* rapidly, in hushed tones. Privately, we assured ourselves that there would be rational explanations for the rattles, bangs, pings, snaps, and creaks: frost popping out nails, wind rattling loose shingles and banging doors we supposed we must have left open, porcupines scrabbling at the foundation, or raccoons or mice or birds or barn cats running across the roof, and so on, if we could just be bothered to sort them out. Besides, if there really were ghosts in the universe, everyone knows, we assured ourselves, that it is *old* buildings that are haunted, not pristine new ones.

But on it went, year after year: strange knockings in or on the walls; abrupt, very loud creaks in the living room's decorative beams; rapid, thunderous banging on the roof that was rather like the sound of a furious workman wielding a hammer. Once, my niece, helping me carry food out to the deck where we were having a barbecue, opened the door to go back into the house just in time to hear a very loud, rapid hammering on the roof. "What was that?" she asked me, frightened. "Oh, nothing. The men," I said tersely, since, on a ranch or a farm, *the men* are always up to something involving hammers, saws, cutting torches, welders, or machines that otherwise make a racket and that *the women* learn to disregard. This apparently satisfied her, even though most, if not all, of "the men" were sitting right there on the deck, glasses of beer in their hands, and I knew it, and I believe she did too. But fortunately, she was still young enough to accept the deliberately chosen, dismissive brusqueness of my tone for authority.

Often in the night dishes rattled in the cupboards as if I had misstacked the plates and they'd suddenly shifted into balance on their own, or we'd be wakened by what sounded like the delicate, clear *ping*ings of water glasses unaccountably striking each other. That was a noise I began to hear in other houses too; once in an eastern city, when my son and I were visiting friends, it seemed as if a tiny, crystal dinner bell was being rung. We were in a large, beautiful house that had been built in the last century, and I imagined when I heard the noise in the dead of night that it was a dainty, feminine spirit wanting to visit me. But by this time I wanted no part of her: *Go away*, I groaned. *I came all this way to escape just this sort of thing.* I think I must have guessed in some mute, subconscious way that having heard one ghost, something in me had opened to let others in.

One night both Peter and I heard heavy footsteps coming up the darkened hall towards our bed, where we lay rigid, waiting for something terrible to happen. But nothing did, and eventually we went back to sleep. Another time I was sure that the blankets covering me were tugged at and pulled off the bed, and my ankle clasped in a heavy hand, but I was so groggy, deep in sleep, that I simply moved my ankle free and kept tugging back on the bedcovers. I don't really know if the bedclothes landed on the floor or, more likely, if the whole thing happened only in some other space of consciousness than the one of real bedclothes and physical ankles.

On another night both of us heard keys rattling at the foot of the bed, and a couple of times the coins that each night Peter empties from his pockets onto the dresser began clinking, as if someone were sorting them in his palm. And once, an invisible person settled heavily down into the chair by the bed with a sigh and a creak as we lay frozen, side by side. *Did you hear that?* we whispered breathlessly to each other.

More often, I would be wakened for no apparent reason and, lying there, I would have the powerful sensation of someone being in the room with us, or several someones, even though I could see well enough in the gloom to know no one corporeal was. Or perhaps I understood on some as-yet-undiscovered psychic level that no one physical was there, that some new sense I hadn't even believed in had for some reason opened up. I remember that on being wakened this way once, I heard suddenly a rapid whispering around all the walls and I felt the whole house shiver—yes, that is the only word I can think of for it—and then a moment later, as happens all the time on the Prairies, a sudden, powerful wind came sweeping from down the valley and began to roar around the house, rattling windows as if trying to climb in and, in a noisy, foul-tempered way, banging objects against the house and deck railing, tumbling them off the deck. It was as if the house had a spirit of its own and had sighed, trembling, bracing itself before the onslaught of the wind only it knew was coming.

And twice that I can recall, we were sitting peacefully reading in the living room in the late evening when both of us heard distinctly three slow knocks on the wall above and behind the sofa. Folklore says that these foretell an imminent death. Indeed, one of these deaths was of my gravely ill mother, the other of a family friend.

Eventually Peter and I gave up pretending it wasn't happening. We no longer bothered to tell ourselves or each other that we were imagining things or that there was no such thing as a ghost or that there was a rational explanation for all the strange noises. By this time it had been going on for so long—and we couldn't explain any of it in a way that we could both agree to—that we simply accepted, with a mixture of resignation, annoyance, and intense curiosity, that we were living in a haunted house.

The river hills sat back of the house, enigmatic, bare of everything but grass and the occasional rock, and coyotes sang to us morning and evening, and mule and white-tailed deer came in bunches down to water at the river, and once a herd of elk, as we stood motionless on the other side, watching them in delight and wonder and with the quiet contentment people get from knowing Nature as the ground of life. At night the Milky Way glittered and gleamed above us, fathomlessly deep and numberless, the constellations wheeled slowly across the sky with the seasons, and the moon came and went, sometimes white as a maiden's face, sometimes a looming orange sphere. Day after day the sun rolled across the heavens and disappeared, only to rise again above the eastern hills. In such a setting, ghosts seemed to us so Old World, so impossibly anachronistic and out of place on the clean, bright prairie and under such an endless, open sky.

Of course, we told nobody—or almost nobody—about the haunting. If a guest remarked on a strange noise when we were sitting in the living room with a drink, we said nothing, or we said, "Yes, this is a noisy house," and changed the subject. Once I said to a visitor, "This house is haunted. Do you believe that?" and waited with bright nervousness for his answer.

"I've never seen a ghost," he said, "but since so many people claim they have, and there have been sightings all over the world, down through all the ages, I'm not about to say they don't exist." I thought that an eminently satisfying answer, and repeat it here, as well as I can remember it, for the benefit of all skeptics.

Why? we asked, when we finally began to talk to each other about it. Why should this be happening while the log house, barely thirty feet away and built before 1912, had never shown any sign of ghosts? Was silent as a tomb at night. We considered the facts. The ground under the new house had never been broken by a plough; there had never been another dwelling on the place where we'd built it. The nearest cemetery was neatly fenced and on the outskirts of town miles away, where the bones of the community's residents dating back to the beginning of this century lay in rows, side by side,

under neat cement blankets and at the foot of simple granite head-
stones: Peter's parents, Alice and George Butala, some of his neighbours from childhood, people who'd died in fires or farm accidents
or in childbirth or quietly in their beds in extreme old age. We even
postulated wildly unsatisfactory theories. Maybe it was the angle
we'd set the house on its foundation—not square to the four directions but aligned roughly northwest to southeast—although what
that might signify or cause, we had no idea. We speculated that
perhaps in some unfathomable way we'd torn the normally elastic
fabric of the universe, allowing another dimension, normally
blocked from us, to flow in.

Nor were our ghosts always frightening. One night when I was
asleep beside him, Peter, who had a severe head cold, woke because
he couldn't breathe, only to find our bedroom filled with an uniden-
tifiable scent—both what it was and where it came from—so
fragrant that it slowly cleared his head and he was able to sleep.

As the years passed—three, then five and seven and ten—we
talked about the reasons for the hauntings, but our discussions
always ended in a heavy, puzzled silence and a turning away to the
dishes that needed washing or to the barn chores that had to be
done. Every once in a while there'd be a long period with no manifestations at all, and I, at least, felt a little disappointed at their
absence and faintly, perversely pleased when the noises returned,
because they were something out of the ordinary and life on a
remote ranch can sometimes be, if not exactly boring, too impersonal, too unstimulating for a woman like me.

The question of who the ghosts might be did not much occupy
us. This was mostly because we could think of absolutely nobody,
none of the unquiet dead, who might belong to us. As for the previous inhabitants of "the valley place," as we sometimes called the hay

farm as another way of distinguishing it from the ranch, forty miles away on the Old Man On His Back plateau, they had been a family to whom not a breath of scandal was attached, good citizens who had lived decently and died well, whom I thought of, although I'd never met them, as being rather like my own grandparents. It seemed to me that the old buildings in which they'd lived and worked, the air of the place itself, had a quiet, peaceable feeling about it. Yet ghosts were surely the souls of dead people, and they had to come from somewhere, they had to have been somebody once, but we could not in our wildest imaginings guess who they might be.

As well, we did not know what the ghosts wanted, what they had against us, if they had anything against us in particular, what they hoped to accomplish by on occasion scaring us half to death—waking us in the dead of night with heavy footsteps coming up the hall towards our bedroom or even waking us just to the very strong sense of other presences in the room with us. But all in all we were not uncheerful; we led a normal life in which the haunting was mostly background (although I was afraid to stay alone there all night, and didn't even like to be alone late in the evening). The whole business was, in general, more annoying than frightening, more irritating than horrifying, eventually more boring than interesting.

Peter and I had married late, he at forty-one and a lifelong bachelor, I at thirty-six, a year or so after my final divorce decree was issued. Having had, for the most part, a long-distance courtship because neither of us could leave our work except for the occasional weekend, we didn't know each other well, and in the first years each of us was a constant surprise to the other. My admiration for Peter—never mind love—deepened with each passing season, and although after the first year I'd stopped accompanying him everywhere, I still helped with the ranch work. In between times I worked part-time as a special-education consultant to the local school districts, and as the years passed, I gradually gave up that work to become a full-time writer, although one who took many days off to help with the big ranching jobs. Our lives seemed full and complete, carried out in a setting of such natural beauty and against the background of the steady round of birth and death and birth again. And each year with the passing of the seasons, the landscape turned from green to gold to white and back to green again. I was learning to think of all this as *the round of being*, a perspective new to me and quietly awe-inspiring to us both, so that when at night there were knocking on the walls, or whispering, or other ghostly manifestations, they didn't upset us unduly.

Besides, although we were scared at times, and thoroughly baffled, we never *saw* a single thing that wasn't really there. Our ghosts did not do anything except call our attention to their presence; they did not actually do any evil that we were aware of. It was as if they were trying to rouse us to something—some kind of action, an awareness of something, some new knowledge—but had no way of telling us what it was they wanted. Whatever that might be, if indeed there was a purpose to their haunting, we could only wait and hope it would be revealed eventually.

In the end, it is true: We did not know why we had ghosts, and we did not know what to do about them.

Wild

Chapter 1

THE FIELD

THE FIRST TIME I SAW THE FIELD WAS SHORTLY AFTER our marriage, when Peter had taken me and some other people from the city there to show us an eagle's nest built high on the steep wall of a coulee. None of us had ever seen an eagle's nest before and we found it a thrilling sight, especially as there were no eaglets in it and we could climb up to it, actually put our hands on its sticks and twigs, and notice how carefully it was constructed using only a slight ledge on the side of the cliff to support its bulk. I'm sure we asked questions, made comments, studied it, before our attention wandered to other nearby, interesting features: the view from that high point, certain plants, maybe an animal sighting.

Peter's father had given him this field when he was eighteen—in his Old-World view, at eighteen a boy became a man. Owning land was part of the definition of "man," and although that particular field was not of much value since it was too hilly and rock-covered ever to be farmed for profit, it was of some use as space and grazing land for cattle and, in practical terms, was necessary for obtaining credit at the bank. Over the years about one hundred acres of the quarter-section (160 acres, or about 73 hectares) had been fenced, and this eventually came to constitute "the field" of this book. Many years later, Peter still cherished it over all the others in his keeping because it was the first land he owned, and because his father had given it to him.

Although for many years there'd been cattle in the field for only a few weeks each spring, about ten years after we married, Peter made the decision to stop putting cattle there. At first it was more by default than design, but then, always deeply interested in prairie ecology, he began to wish to see what the field would look like if it were left alone for a substantial length of time. When I first saw the field that day so long ago now, it was most striking for its barrenness, its roughness, and for the scrubby nature of what growth was there. I felt it had great beauty, but it was a strange, austere beauty.

After that day, I began to walk there often by myself. I liked being in that field. I liked the way the terrain changed and changed again whether I walked north or south or east or west, from the steep cliffside where the eagles' nest for years had hung, to the low grasscovered flat areas, to the places where nothing grew because there was only hardpan—clay so fine-grained that precipitation collected in its depressions would evaporate before it was absorbed. There was a place where a jumble of rocks, all sizes, shapes, and colours, for no reason I could see, lay carelessly tumbled about. I liked the scent in the air of sage and creeping juniper, of wild roses, and of the many different grasses with their more subtle fragrances. It seemed to me that the air was fresher and cleaner there and had a tang in it missing from the sweet-smelling cultivated hay fields, the cropland, or the seeded, mown, and watered grass of the front lawns and parks with which I was so familiar.

There was not one tree in the field. I asked what had created this varied and often harsh terrain and was told that the glaciers had scraped down this area, melting back about twelve thousand years ago. As they retreated they took nearly all the topsoil with them, hence the relatively sparse vegetation and probably the lack of trees. They left behind many feet of glacial till, rocks that had dropped from the melting ice, some enormous, many of which had come from hundreds of miles away. The nearly mile-wide section of the Frenchman River valley where we had built our house was once a huge glacial spillway, but now had only a narrow little river wending its way through it. The only trees were a few willows growing along the riverbanks, although where there had been settlers were rows of poplars or cottonwoods and caragana around the houses.

I used to "save" that field for days when I was completely alone—Peter off on business elsewhere, the hired man away, and no neighbours or friends about or expected. Then I could close the door and set off alone or with our collies Prince and Rover (as the years passed, the dogs changed) for a couple of solitary hours wandering in the field, for although it was my practice to walk every day for the sake of fitness, I never went to the field with that in mind. It was just a way, on one of the many days I was alone, to pass the time in an environment that pleased me more than walking in other fields or down the road or driving into town or, unable to settle down to read or write, pacing at home from room to room, bored and yearning for congenial company.

Although going there always took some effort, since it was a long walk and summer here on the northern Great Plains is typically, unbearably hot, I liked being there enough to put on my wide-brimmed hat and set off anyway. There was something about that field, though, that made me approach it with a measure of apprehension. It wasn't anything I could put my finger on, or that made any sense to me beyond the field's wildness, and so I thought I was being silly and that my silliness was born of my twenty-some years as a city-dweller, even though I'd lived in small towns before that and, from my birth until school age, in the bush country of northern Saskatchewan.

Peter liked the field for the same reasons I did. Because it was grazed by cattle for only a few weeks in the spring, had never been ploughed—*could* never be ploughed because of its rough terrain—and nobody but us ever went there, on horseback or on foot, we felt as if we had gone back a hundred years to the time before the first settlers (when we would have had to be on our guard for marauding plains grizzly bears and prairie wolves, now extinct). Or even five hundred years, before horses had reached the northern plains. Maybe even two thousand years ago, when the earth was what it was—an earth we ecologically minded folk now like to imagine, probably foolishly, as Eden. (A far cry from the visionary poet William Blake who wrote, "Where man is not, nature is barren." But then, he lived all his life in London.) We liked the field's silence too, which I noticed early on. Although it seemed strange, eerie even, to be far from buildings and traffic and yet to hear little or no birdsong or the chirps, clicks, and whirrs of insects, I was so unfamiliar with this prairie that it didn't occur to me to question why it had no noises beyond the yodelling of coyotes.

Probably the first spring of our marriage, Peter had been out checking cattle on horseback and had brought me back a small cluster of crocuses. He'd found them in the field, he said, and after that, every spring as the snow began to melt, I would make a pilgrimage there to look for crocuses. (Here it's a matter of pride to be among the first to have a small bouquet of the wild, yellow-centred, mauve and purple flowers, actually anemones, sitting on the kitchen table.) As the years passed and I became familiar with the climate and the weather, I became more and more accurate in my guess as to the day they would first bloom, and as the frigid winter days began to warm and the sun to set later, I would wait impatiently till the time was right to make my pilgrimage.

As I came to know the field better I would watch for whatever plants came next in the season—the fragile pale-pink-to-rose gumbo evening primroses that would spring up amazingly in soil where nothing else would grow, the frilled, delicate lemon-yellow blooms of the prickly pear cactus, and the spiky, bright fuchsia ones of the pincushion cactus, the tiny scarlet mallow that my books said was sacred to the goddess. These were the most obvious plants, aside from the various kinds of wild asters and daisy-like plants whose names I didn't know and whose blooms were yellow or white or mauve. Even though much of the field had growing on it only sage, patches of cactus, greasewood, or badger bush (south of here called buck brush but, more properly, snowberry), there were also, among many other indigenous grasses, good-sized stands of blue grama grass, a particularly distinctive and attractive shortgrass that always delighted me to find. Under and around the grass, especially on the very dry hillsides with their thin covering of light brown soil, I would find patches of moss, one of Nature's ways, I was told, of preventing erosion in such vulnerable spots, and another moss-like plant which I discovered would bloom early in the year with a surprising profusion of tiny white flowers.

I had come from the parkland area in Saskatchewan and north of there in bush country, and I was used to a much different terrain, as well as to rich black soil in which crops and vegetable and flower gardens flourished with little effort, accustomed to tall, thick stands of green grass and bigger, brighter, more abundant wildflowers, such as our provincial flower, the tiger, or Western red, lily. Here in this field with its products of a different climate and different soil, I was discovering Nature at work in a more precise fashion, producing a finely articulated array of plants that required close attention to be appreciated.

You could be pretty sure of animal sightings too. There were many deer and coyote trails, and in the years when there were jackrabbits, their trails were evident going straight over even the highest hills, never around them. If you looked closely, you could see the tiny paths of field mice, insects, and even snakes. More than once, walking too near a clump of silver sage, its greyed woody stems twisted and splintered with age, I startled a half-dozen garter snakes into a quick exit into holes under its roots. Twice I found tiny, perfect kangaroo mice lying dead on my path, as if they'd had heart attacks or had lain down quietly and died of old age. Exploring the field by myself once, on a cliffside I discovered what I was sure was a bobcat den—I could smell them—and thought the wisest course was to back away quickly.

I used to come upon a badger there. I can't say I ever saw his eyes, and he certainly never made a sound, but I could feel how profoundly it irritated him that he'd been seen at all, and he'd waddle rapidly away out of sight. Badgers are notoriously private and solitary, and also very grouchy, and I always felt embarrassed when I saw him, as if I'd tried to get into an already-occupied phone booth by mistake and should apologize, knowing full well no apology could possibly suffice to somebody so out of love with humanity.

For a long time, too, a pair of golden eagles lived in the nest on the cliffside. If you saw one of them in the blue high above you, you had only to look around to find the other, the two of them sailing high above in wide interlocking circles, a hunting pattern, sometimes casting a great shadow as one of them fell through layers of sky to plane low over the grass and rocks where movement had caught its eagle's eye.

Then, one day, walking the field with my son and daughter-in-law, we descended a rugged, juniper-covered slope and there we found, just outside a hole in the crumbling clay side of the hill and by a large rock, the feathers and claws of a large bird we thought was probably an eagle. It was freshly killed by a coyote, we guessed, which had perhaps lain there in wait for it but more likely by sheer serendipity had been there when the eagle had descended on prey. Knowing eagle feathers are held to be sacred in Plains Amerindian culture, we gathered them carefully and took them home, but not knowing that the claws are also greatly valued, thinking them grotesque, we left them behind. A couple of weeks later, rethinking this, I went back but couldn't find them, couldn't even find with certainty the exact spot where the great bird had been killed. And after that, there was only one golden eagle as resident of the field.

More than once, lifting my eyes from the ground and looking around, I spotted a lone coyote sitting on a hill high above me, silently watching me. I often saw coyotes trotting their trails to or from their dens, their noses to the ground, their tails brushing the earth behind them. When they saw me, they would pause, sit back on their haunches, abruptly swinging their heads to nose a flea on a flank and then turning back to me, and finally, after consideration, sounding not very alarmed, begin yipping or yodelling. I was nervous of them, although I loved their singing, but they always kept their distance, even when they followed me, and I grew to enjoy their presence too. Sooner or later they grew bored, trotted off behind a hill, and didn't reappear.

I startled deer out of comfortable resting spots high in the clefts of coulees where, lying in the patches of badger bush and wild rosebushes, they blended into the landscape. Or I would often come upon the small basins of grass pressed flat by their bodies where they'd been lying. I learned that they chose spots where they'd be warm but not too hot from the sun and where they had a good view of the countryside. On windy days, walking among scatterings of rocks on gravelly ground, I startled small birds out of their shelters in the still places where several rocks nested against each other.

None of this was earth-shattering; none of it would have surprised any wildlife expert, or botanist or biologist, or even any farm- or ranch-raised child. Having seen it, none of them would be writing a book about it. I can't honestly say that it even surprised me, my earliest memories being of earth and grass and trees. But now I was seeing all this, for the most part, alone, at my own speed, in my own way, as an adult. No one was telling me what to look at, or explaining it to me, or telling me to wait and look longer, or not to bother looking at this or that. This, it was now beginning to seem to me, had been the story of my entire life up to that point, the assumption by everyone significant to me apparently having been that I wasn't clever enough or sensible enough to know what I ought to be looking at or, worse, that I didn't have the right to choose for myself. In the midst of the severe difficulties of adjustment I was trying to deal with, having moved here from Saskatoon where I had been a graduate student and lowly lecturer in the College of Education at the University of Saskatchewan, the simple fact of finding once again what I liked myself, something which I'd long since lost track of in my first disastrous marriage, was a quiet joy.

Nor did I have to rush home to do the housework, or make the endless phone calls for the volunteer work I used to do, or get to my job, or do the tasks that I hadn't managed to finish at work, or spend time with my child (he was going to high school in the city and living with his father and new stepmother and spending his long weekends and holidays with me), or do the washing, or the never-ending tasks of a modern woman's life. I walked and I looked, by myself, taking my own good time, and in that solitary walking and looking, I found a new world that I would otherwise never have seen. Even now I'm surprised by the great and continuing pleasure that discovering the life of Nature holds for me.

One day, walking in the field, I found a stone circle, a tepee ring, as everyone calls them. I wasn't surprised, since by then I knew that these stone rings are on nearly all the unploughed land of the southwest, but I was pleased with myself because I was pretty sure that Peter didn't know it was there, or he'd have shown it to me, and that anyone else who knew about it was almost certainly long dead. Walking the field that summer and the next, I found a few more small stone circles. In a world in which I did not fit, had no friends or family, knew little about how it functioned and consequently was alone far more than I wanted to be, I had found something on my own, and although I didn't directly realize it then, this discovery gave me something solid and understandable to hold on to. Thus was the beginning of making the place my own.

Often I would go slightly beyond the field's borders, paying more attention to its natural contours as markers than to the irrelevant and annoying fencelines. This was how, a slight distance away from the field's fenceline, I discovered groupings of tepee rings. Because by this time I was reading books for laypeople about the archeology of the northern Great Plains, I recognized them clearly by their size and their arrangement as the remains of an encampment. I would never know how big the camp had been, because the rest of the field was ploughed, nor had I any way of telling how old the rings were or whether they'd all been made at the same time or over ten or twenty thousand years. But I was deeply pleased by what I'd found, and walked among the rings considering them with wonder and excitement.

One day it occurred to me to imagine myself an Amerindian woman perhaps two thousand years ago, who had broken camp and was moving on to the next one. I imagined myself on foot, carrying objects, perhaps even had a child on my back. I walked from the encampment I'd found, imagining I was moving west with my people, down the slope, and then hesitated. What path would I choose from here? Common sense dictated that I wouldn't climb any hills I could avoid, and simple caution would mean I probably wouldn't want to be visible from a great distance as enemies might be about. Probably I would take to the draws between hills.

I picked my way carefully, planning ahead. In the first draw I stopped. There on a flat area on my left was a tepee ring I hadn't seen before. It was a shock, the kind of shock the *I Ching* speaks of:

Shock comes—oh, oh!
Laughing words—ha, ha!

My heart felt as if it had jumped into my throat. The tepee ring was exactly where it would need to be if my guesses about all the contingencies of the hypothetical woman's passage were correct. I walked farther, found several more tepee rings just where they would be if people had passed this way. My excitement was great. For the first time in my life *I felt the past speaking to me.*

Meditating over the days that followed on the plan I'd made and the discovery that resulted from it, I thought to myself: If I walk this field enough and think about it enough, it will teach me the past. I meant by this that I would not dig into the ground as an archeologist does; I would not even talk to an archeologist for clues. (In any event, at that time, I knew no archeologists.) I would just walk and think and study what was there, and in time the meaningful pattern I felt sure was there would become evident to me. Or if not a pattern, I would find clues that would make the actual events that happened here clear to me. I didn't know exactly what it was I was seeking, although I thought it was something concrete, a history, a sociology, the life story of a people.

I was finding stone circles here and there all over the field; I kept stumbling across them in the grass as I wandered. Some of them I'd find one day and then couldn't find the next time I looked for them. My guess was that they became visible some days with a certain slant of light and disappeared back into the grass or into what became merely a confusion of stones when the light was different, or appeared and disappeared at other times of day with the changing light. This I knew about with regard to petroglyphs, which can best be seen, or sometimes only seen, near sunrise and sunset when the light is long and slanting, casting strong shadows. Although I sometimes blamed my inability to find their exact location on my bad memory, I also considered that probably I wasn't looking for them at the right time of day. Nonetheless, I thought, if there were stone circles, people had been here, and people left behind clues to their presence: points, flakes, tools, pots, bones, even graves. I began to look more seriously.

At first, having no better idea, I wanted to find arrowheads and spear points, but finding points is a gift which, sadly, I soon came to realize I don't have. (To this day, despite months of looking, I've never found one.) Instead I found tools or, more often, the remains of tool-making, what archeologists call "flakes." Those I found—I wasn't always sure if they were remains or the actual tools, but preferred to think they were the latter—were probably designed for the scraping of hides; I say this because of the way they fit my hand, so that I could imagine myself drawing them carefully, firmly but gently, down a hide, and that meant that women had used them (although I supposed that men had made them). I found many others whose use was less clear to me, and some of which looked to me like either badly made or unfinished tools, perhaps abandoned by their makers as unsatisfactory, perhaps broken in the making. Nearly all of these are made of chert, most of which is an unattractive dull tan colour, often with a centre of opaque bluish grey.

I began to see that the women liked to sit on low hills to do their work, where they would be in the breeze, be cooler, and perhaps find some relief from mosquitoes and flies, perhaps enjoy being a little higher than the rest of the world. I discovered this because on low, grassy hills I nearly always found scrapers or flakes, but never on patches of hardpan or poor soil where only greasewood and cactus grew, and not on the crumbling clay sides of steep coulees. But a smooth, grassy patch on a low or moderately high hilltop, yes, all the time.

At first I brought some of these home with me, but eventually I gave that up, partly because I learned it was against the law to remove them but mostly because it began to seem a senseless thing to do. What were they to do cluttering up my shelves and growing dusty? What was I trying to prove by bringing them home (and three or four years later being unable to remember precisely where I'd found them—an archeologist's nightmare)? I began to pick them up in order to study them, but then I'd put them back precisely in their little burrows, nestled in the moss or forming a clear, dark shape in the soil, where they'd come from. Then, when I came upon them again, it was like coming across a friend.

One day as I was walking an area of small, low hills, I found a white quartz sphere about the size of a billiard ball that looked to me to have been chipped by a human hand into its spherical shape. I had learned that when I found flakes, often if I looked only a foot or two away, I would locate the remainder of the rock from which the flake had been broken and could make the pieces more or less fit together. Since the sphere was a surprising finding, I looked around, and a few feet away, I located a white quartz cylinder about six inches long and an inch or less in diameter. It seemed clear that the two belonged together, although I had no idea what their use might have been. Ceremonial, I wondered? For ritual of some sort? Or maybe they were parts of a game? I couldn't recall ever having seen anything in my brief reading of archeological literature about objects like these.

I suppose because it had become my habit not to take things away from the field, I left the quartz shapes where I found them. But I kept thinking about them, and away from them and the field they seemed to me even more remarkable. Inevitably, I eventually went back to find them again. I remembered exactly where they'd been—the precise hill, the correct side of the hill, the place on the hill where I'd picked them up.

I searched that small area for a couple of hours, then expanded my search several feet in each direction, without finding them. They simply were not there. I went back three or four times on other days over the following months and each time searched the area with great care, and when I still did not find them, I expanded my search to a wider area and examined all of it minutely and, when I still didn't find them, tried neighbouring hills in case I'd made so elementary a mistake as to have remembered the wrong hill. But the white stone sphere and the stone stick were nowhere, had vanished, disappeared off the earth.

One day, a week or more after the original find, searching the original location, I found two stone artifacts that might once have been, more or less, a white stone sphere and a white stone stick. They were hardly identifiable, chipped and misshapen with growths, discoloured by contact with the earth and plants, and overgrown with lichen, a far cry from the pristine white sphere and ball I remembered holding in my hands. Perhaps these two dubious objects I was holding now were indeed the same ones, but a thousand or two thousand years after their fashioning. I could not decide what to make of them, and finally, deeply perplexed, I set them back where I'd found them and continued my search for the "real" ones.

Still determined that they were there and that I would find them if I were dogged enough in my search, that if I wanted them badly enough the sphere and the cylinder could be made to reappear, I kept looking with an intensity that had gone beyond common sense, when suddenly a question popped sharply into my head—as if there'd been a speaker—asking, *What do you want them for?*

I was shaken. For what indeed did I so badly want them? Oh! I said to myself, in surprise and dismay: I want them only out of stubbornness, out of curiosity, to add them to my collection of flakes that sit purposelessly on my shelves, or maybe to show them to an archeologist one day. I don't want them *for* anything. Understanding now that while they were objects of great curiosity to me, for those who had left them behind they meant a great deal more, even if I had no idea just what. Chastened and, at back of it, profoundly puzzled, I gave up my quest. But even now, years later, whenever I cross that hill I make another cursory search, just in case. And now it occurs to me to wonder what made me leave them behind that first day, what made me leave behind so startling a find.

Imagine me as a small, aging, not very strong woman in apparently perfect health, having walked away from everything that, presumably, meant something to me. Imagine me alone, year after year, mutely longing for all I'd left behind, suppressing the longing, never speaking of it, contemplating leaving year after year, and year after year staying. For although I was unhappy, it was not anybody's fault that I was. I simply couldn't find firm ground on which to stand. And it wasn't endless, hopeless misery but, instead, a kind of unhappiness that held promise of one day bearing fruit.

I was, I think in retrospect, caught in some huge spiritual emptiness, all my old ideas about life and how to live it in which I'd been raised having turned out to be a total failure, a sham and a lie, and yet I had nothing else to take their place. How could I go back to nothing? I needed to re-create myself, and I did not know what that was or how to do it or even that that was what I was trying to do. I walked the prairie, I studied it, I talked to myself, I read books, I considered the horned lark who never considered me, and the badger who snarled at me, and the calves who gambolled on dainty hooves in the spring, their white faces shining like pretty white daisies in the grass, and the hawks that circled and shrieked, and the long, wavering V's of geese coming and going so mysteriously. I learned that skunks lived in every stone pile, that insects survived in all the cracks of earth and buildings, that birds seemed to come from nowhere if I sprinkled water on the crested wheatgrass that formed our lawn. It was all a revelation to me, one that rested, I was finding, on the bedrock of mystery.

In the field now, I had found one arrangement of stones that was not enigmatic as to its shape and location and that did not have the annoying habit of appearing and disappearing. It was always there, on a long, narrow hill with a flattish top, of medium height, in a prominent place in the field. I had discovered in other fields that the stone circles that weren't clearly tepee rings (although what they were nobody knew) often were arranged along a sloping hill, but always stopped short before the highest point. This particular hill had no highest point, was closer to being a wide, flattened ridge, a miniature plateau with, on one side, a sharp drop-off, and on the other, a gradual slope to lower ground. This flattened ridge seemed to attract an approach from the long west end, although for years I approached it willy-nilly from whatever direction I happened to be coming.

On top of the miniature plateau and at the west end was a large circle of embedded stone (the fact that they were embedded in the ground signified that the circle had been made a long, but indefinite time earlier). It was perhaps four times as large as the stone circles elsewhere in the field or near it that were clearly the tepee rings of a small family. West of the circle was a north-south line of embedded stone, and east of it, near the centre of the plateau, was a grouping of larger stones, the bottom ones embedded and the upper ones not. The large stone circle also had a pile of mostly embedded stones on the perimeter of the circle, at what I guessed to be roughly each of the four directions.

I had read enough by now to speculate that this might be, perhaps—I was not at all certain—the burial tent of a Blackfoot chief. At that time I had read archeology, not ethnology, and I didn't know the simplest thing, such as that a leader might have a larger lodge than other members of his people or that ceremonies, indicated by the piles of stones at the four directions, were routinely carried on in such tepees. I simply thought such a large circle had to be something important, and I knew that the people my history books called "the Blackfoot" (their correct name is *Siksika)*—now a confederacy of several peoples of whom the Siksika is only one—who had hunted in this area in the nineteenth century, would sometimes perform ceremonies and then leave a dead leader in his lodge and come back later for his bones and bury them.

I had no idea what the other stones on the plateau were for, but having been "arranged" or "culturally modified," as the archeologists say, they seemed to me to carry meaning, even if I couldn't read it. Off-centre inside the large circle was a small circle of embedded stone, perhaps for a cooking fire or maybe an altar or a fire connected with ceremonies, I didn't know which.

I wanted to know more. During this time I was lucky enough to be a member of our provincial Heritage Foundation Board, where I picked up some miscellaneous information about the Amerindians of the past in what is now Saskatchewan and where I had the good fortune to get to know an archeologist who also sat on the board. He gave me clues as to what to look for in my rambles across our land. When I told him about a certain glacial erratic high on a hill, the only one for miles in any direction, he suggested I might try looking for beads or other offerings in its long, deep cracks. But when I asked him about the stone circle and the other piles of stone on the long, flat hill, he was noncommittal about their possible meaning, and so my sense of mystery grew, and with it my desire to understand the meaning of the stone arrangements I was finding.

Some strange physical thing was happening to me. I was losing energy. I could hardly walk a half-mile before my strength gave way and I was overcome by an exhaustion that made it hard for me to breathe, my lungs burned with it, and my whole body, every muscle, was saturated with tiredness. I felt I couldn't lift my leg to take one more step; I wanted only to fall to the ground and lie there motionless until it seeped away again. It differed from normal tiredness, caused by lack of sleep or by doing too much physically—walking too far or doing spring housecleaning or dancing all night. That kind of tiredness is in a sense enjoyable, even welcome, and it leads to sleep or to a comfortable rest from which one rises refreshed. This tiredness felt more like a tide of illness sweeping through my body, manifesting itself as physical exhaustion, although it wasn't accompanied by nausea or any other symptom.

It was very unpleasant, it restricted me somewhat, feeling at times that I couldn't take another step, and it scared me, but I didn't go to a doctor. I pointed out to myself that I had no other symptoms: I wasn't losing weight, I had a good appetite, and anything physical I wanted to do I could always, eventually, even if only bit by bit, find the energy for. And usually, too, although not always, I didn't feel this terrible exhaustion when I was away in the city, or farther, in other provinces. I concluded it surely had to be caused by my psychological struggles, my unhappiness and uncertainty about my new life in this new country, and by the books I was reading that told me I knew nothing and was a sinner and had barely opened myself to the world of the spirit, which was where I had to go to survive but didn't know if I had the courage. I also thought that it was probably caused by my struggles to become a writer, my great desire that seemed to me to be constantly frustrated by circumstances—how far I lived from other writers and the writing world, the inevitable, but nonetheless debilitating rejections, my sense that the words I struggled so hard over would remain unread or, if read, would never be attended to or valued.

At some point, I realized that I most clearly suffered from my exhaustion when I was going for walks. But why, I wondered, when walks were my chief joy, recreation, and solace? Looking back, I am sure that when for a couple of years I had a woman-friend, I didn't suffer from my exhaustion if I walked with her. But when we walked together, I realized, we didn't leave the roads. I began to suspect that my extreme exhaustion was somehow connected to the field.

As I've said, I didn't go to the doctor. When it was too cold out for weeks at a time or too wet for walking on our gumbo soils, when I had flu or a cold or was away from home or at home but too busy and thus wasn't walking, I would forget about this inexplicable, occasional dysfunction. When on a walk it would return, leaving me standing in the middle of a field perplexed and depressed, I would think only of getting home or to my destination, and after my brief pause to rest, I'd be able to do so. I had no doubt that if I went to the doctor, he would not be able to find a physical cause and would dismiss me as just another baffling and annoying middle-aged-female hypochondriac. I couldn't stand the thought of that humiliation. How I knew this wasn't a physical ailment, or why I was so sure this was the case, I cannot explain. I can only say I felt that my exhaustion when walking was an infirmity with a spiritual or a psychological basis, one which carried meaning that I had not, as yet, deciphered but one that was my duty, and mine alone, to understand and deal with. I think that Jungian analysts, at least, will here nod wisely in agreement with me, and they will not be surprised when I say that this condition went on for years.

I'd been suffering from it perhaps seven or more years when finally I decided I needed to at least try to take control of my own life. I would give in and go to the doctor. I made an appointment, I sat in his anteroom an hour waiting for my turn, and then, when there was only one more patient ahead of me, I got up and went home, and I didn't return. Nor did I tell anybody.

During all of this, of course, life went on. I settled again into the world of the married. Peter and I drove to town or to Medicine Hat or Swift Current or to Havre, Montana, went to friends' houses for dinner with other couples or invited them to ours, or went to the wedding dances and the twenty-fifth anniversary celebrations or to events in town. I helped by chasing cows on horseback or by cooking meals for crews invited in to do the big jobs like branding and vaccinating the cattle. Evenings we watched television and went to bed, and in the morning got up and listened to the birds singing in the poplars around our house. The sun rose and set and rose again.

In the fall we saw the ducks and geese passing over, and in the spring searched out the place where the sage hens danced, or we crouched low on the bank of a slough, hiding behind the tall grasses, to watch the wild swans gliding over the water. Peter fed cows all winter in the snow and cold, and I cooked big meals to keep him going. Sometimes I drove the tractor or a truck for him as he forked hay off the flat deck for cattle, or stamped my feet in the cold to keep them warm as I opened and closed gates to let him on his tractor in or out of the corrals while preventing any animals from escaping. I helped in small ways with the spring calving—holding ropes, adding my small strength to his to pull the occasional calf, driving the truck with a sick calf in the box while he rode horseback behind its mother as we brought them into the barn for treatment. Otherwise I stayed at home and wrote books and read them and, in my loneliness, walked and walked and walked, and thought.

The Field

One year on the evening of the summer solstice, I went with Peter just before sunset to the field. We sat on the west end of a long hill, Peter on a rock and me on my knees in the sparse grass, watching the sun go down. It was perfectly still, not a sound, not so much as a breath of wind, and the blaze of rose-gold light only slightly occluded by low cloud so thin as to be almost a vapour.

On my knees, I looked at the patch of ground around me strewn with small red, beige, white, and black stones, covered with patches of pale green, russet, and black lichen; at least a dozen different kinds of short plants, some grasses, some flowering plants, most of which I couldn't name, were growing in and around and underneath the stones, and here and there little clumps of grey-green club moss. In the strong, low light from the west I was stunned by the beauty of this small piece of the earth and by its diversity. I said to Peter, "And we think this land barren and useless!"

He turned on his stone stool and looked down at the patch of earth I was studying, and we talked about how sad it is that our agriculture wastes all this bounty without ever knowing what it is, and especially, thinking it valueless, how it destroys this blessed beauty.

The light intensified the colours, gave strength and clarity to each outline of plant and stone, lent them a kind of superreality and a stunning beauty that made me want to paint them, to sing them in song, to take a photograph of them and hang it on my wall; it made me want to cherish them as precious beyond words, to tell everyone in the world to look, only *look*.

Subtly, without my fully, clearly noticing it, the field had gone from being an aesthetically pleasing, interesting, and refreshing place in Nature to walk to a place that spoke to and soothed my often weary spirit, if not my frequently exhausted body. It had begun to take the place of the friends who were all far away, of the teachers and counsellors I didn't have, of the family I had left behind when I had married. It didn't occur to me that this was odd.

As I walked the field and the years passed, I began to think that I knew its terrain pretty well, that I knew what animals I might see there and how they might behave. I'd never seen a bobcat in the field, but I had seen a young one once a few miles away, and once in the soft darkness of a summer night as Peter and I lay in bed, we heard one scream not far from our open window. Otherwise, as the years went by, I no longer expected surprises in the field.

One day, I took a new friend there for a walk. We climbed the steep side of a cliff, at the top sauntered along a little way, then, tired by our ascent since we're both aging women, we descended the slope again a few feet to a large, flat dolomite rock, where we sat and continued our conversation. My friend sat below looking up, and I sat at the top of the rock looking down at her.

We'd been there maybe five minutes when suddenly I saw something below and behind her; I jumped to my feet and started down the hill. There, on an earth ledge, lay the largest snake I have ever seen in the flesh, perhaps six feet long, four inches in diameter at its thickest part, and beautifully striped from its head to its tail in alternating, concentric cream and brown rings each about an inch and a half wide. Although there are not supposed to be rattlesnakes in this area, my friend and I were nonetheless wary, staying a respectful, not to say timorous, eight feet away, guessing, hoping, that it was a bull or gopher snake.

Eventually—since snakes can't hear as we do—our footfalls must have alerted it to our presence. As we watched, both scared and delighted, the snake, without the slightest acknowledgement of our presence, unwound its loops in a measured, leisurely way and slid down inch by inch into a snug hole in the cliffside. Later, my friend said, "It was then I noticed that there were holes just like it all around us!"

When I first came here, I was told that bull snakes were a part of this ecology but that they were so shy or rare, or both, I'd never see one. Peter has lived here his entire life and never has, and in fact, I know few local people who ever have. Because they were so seldom seen, without realizing it I had relegated them to the realm of the mythical. Now, just when I was beginning to think I'd pretty much seen all there was to see in the field, the landscape had opened another crack to reveal one more of its secrets.

My immediate feeling was triumphant—now I *had* seen everything. But almost at once that sense of triumph dwindled and then dissipated, replaced by a steadily growing uneasiness. I had been opened to the field again, my sense of wonder renewed, and I found myself speculating about what more there might be here that I hadn't seen, didn't know about, had not even guessed at. Now, slowly, I began to conceive of the field in an entirely new way; I began to understand it as *layers of presence* gradually disclosing themselves to me. And I couldn't help but wonder, if I had the patience, the curiosity, and a quiet sense of the holy, what more the field might still have to reveal.

Chapter 2

ABUNDANCE

WHEN I BEGAN TO KNOW THAT THE FIELD HELD MANY Amerindian artifacts, I at first hoped to find spear points or arrowheads. I know someone who can always find them and who, on the evidence of what he has told me about how he does it, seems to enter something of an altered state to know where they are. I learned to recognize scrapers and flakes and can find scrapers as easily as snow in a prairie winter, but after much fruitless searching, I've finally had to accept that I just don't have the gift for finding points. When I had concluded that I never would, I shifted my desire to a speculative idea of learning something of the prairie plants about which Amerindian people were so knowledgeable.

Farming and ranching people, with their ideas of land use brought with their grandparents from Europe, had defined the field as barren and useless. To Peter and me, knowing a little about the Amerindian past, it was not barren because it was beautiful, and to us, beauty was a use, and a very important one, more important even than grazing or crop-growing. But we didn't have any practical knowledge or experience as to what would make it, in its natural state, a place where one might sustain life in the purely physical sense. I thought it would be interesting, and possibly enlightening, to know something about the plants in the field.

Probably because it was supposed to be everywhere, I fixed my imagination on Indian breadroot (*Psoralea esculenta*), also called prairie turnip, which sounded about my speed and which was said to be a part of the Plains Amerindian diet. For a very long time it was in the back of my mind that one day I would look up Indian breadroot and then go out and find it. But I never seemed to remember to look it up ahead of time or to bring a plant book with me to the field, and as I walked the prairie or sat on the grass contemplating the fields and hills, I sometimes wondered idly what it looked like and which of the many plants around me it might be.

For a long time historians interested in Amerindians of the Plains focused on the buffalo and the culture that grew up around them. Most likely, the locating of the buffalo, the chase, the kill were all so dramatic, so heroic that they captured the imagination of the chiefly male researchers, who didn't bother to consider non-buffalo-influenced life. Finally, a closer look has been taken at the diet of Plains Amerindians, and now it is said that plant foods, from berries to leaves and roots, all harvested on the common prairie, were a vital and substantial part of their food. I'd read that among the Peigan, a member of the Blackfoot Confederacy, root vegetables accounted for one-third of the plant foods in their diet.

"Root vegetables," I thought, probably means Indian breadroot, which had been the most important of the wild foods harvested by Plains people. In terms of its nutritional value, it's reported to contain 66.6 grams of carbohydrates per 100 grams fresh weight, has more protein in it than a comparable amount of potato, and is also a good source of vitamin C.

I wondered when to look for it, that is, when it would be ready to harvest, and on this point my sources differed. One said spring—it must have been late spring when the root would have been fresh and tender—but other sources say it was a late-summer-to-fall vegetable. To harvest it, the women sharpened a digging stick, most often of birch, saskatoon, or chokecherry wood, carefully rounded at the pushing end to aid in prying the long root out of the ground. Apparently every Cree woman carried one with her all summer long, and this suggests that the women took the plant when and where they could find it.

Freshly dug, peeled, and chopped, prairie turnip was added to meat stews, or it was baked or boiled, or pounded and used as a thickening agent in soups. The Cree ground it into meal and made cakes that were baked over coals, or else they mixed it with flour and berries and made a pudding. If it was to be preserved for winter use, it was peeled and dried whole, or several were braided together and dried, or it was peeled, sliced, threaded on sinew string, and hung out to dry in the sun.

Not only was Indian breadroot a vital nutritional source, but it had a number of medicinal uses, from chewing the leaves for sore throat (Arapaho and Siksika)—although another source says that for the same purpose the Peigan brewed the root and drank the tea—to chewing the root and applying the result to sprains and broken bones and, especially, to eyes (all my sources agree on this one), where it was an aid in removing foreign matter.

But its importance is validated by another fact: Indian breadroot had a prominent use in the spiritual ceremonies of some Plains people. In the sun dance of the Peigan people, a sacred digging stick and a "holy turnip" bundle are involved. This ritual is conducted by a woman as a symbol for "Holy Woman," who first dug the turnip, which was given to her by the Moon. On reading this fact, I thought I really must look the plant up. But still, there was so much to see in the field, so much of interest, that I never seemed to get around to it.

I felt fairly sure that the plant existed in the field, as I'd found so many other signs of Amerindian life in it. Now, having found out how important Indian breadroot once was, I was embarrassed to think that I'd lived on the Saskatchewan prairie all but five years of my life and yet wouldn't know Indian breadroot if I fell over it. Nor could anyone else I know identify it, including my mother who, when we were children, used to send us out in the spring to harvest young dandelion greens for salad. We picked berries, saskatoons, and chokecherries especially, but also pincherries, gooseberries, and north of here, in the fields and forests of my childhood, blueberries, and wild strawberries, out of which every household made gallons of syrup, jams, and jellies or, in later years, froze them for pies and puddings. And yet no one knew, often didn't even know *of*, Indian breadroot.

It seemed to me thick-headed of us all, in that the first settlers here had a very hard struggle. Whole families survived all winter on nothing but potatoes and became ill and died or went crazy and yet, with the exception of berries, seemed not to have turned to Amerindian sources of plant food. All of my grandparents were settlers—one of my grandfathers was said to have been born under the wagonbox at Portage la Prairie on the trek west from Ontario in 1884—and yet it seems that all my clever and resourceful mother knew about indigenous food, she who had for some years lived merely yards away from Amerindian encampments as the men worked in my father's sawmill, was to pick dandelion greens.

Maybe this failure had its roots in excessive ethnocentricity: that the settlers thought of themselves as the enlightened who were bringing civilization to the wild Prairies. They thought, too, that they could merely transplant their own cultures here, that hard work and ingenuity were all that were required to make the prairie bloom like an English or a French garden, or to produce a vegetable garden to feed a family for a year as they could easily have done in the milder climate of Ukraine or other central European countries, there lacking only the land to do so. That the people native to this continent might know valuable things about how to make a life here on the Prairies, for the most part, never seems to have entered most of their heads. Of course, the first step to bringing settlers to the West was to impoverish and vanquish the Amerindians, moving them all onto reserves where their contacts with the new arrivals were reduced to an absolute minimum. So perhaps no Amerindian people were available to most of the settlers for advice.

Day after day I walked the field and thought about things like this, and gradually it began to dawn on me that it was both amazing and shameful that I was still in many ways as ignorant of this land as my great-grandparents had been when they arrived from Ireland and Scotland in the mid-nineteenth century and, two centuries before that, from France. Yet, looking around the field, I certainly couldn't see how people could find enough plant food here to sustain life, or even what plants they might eat beyond berries and Indian breadroot.

Certain flowers, however, we non-Amerindians are experts on. Crocuses, for example, are one of the few prairie plants that have been a part of my life as far back as I can remember, no matter whether I lived in Saskatchewan's bush country, the parkland region, or down here in the southwest. Not only are they pretty, but they give no difficulty in identification, they arrive so early as to be the first true sign that the long winter is over, and there is always a touch of the miraculous about them because they often bloom only inches away from a snowbank. All prairie people have great affection for crocuses. In homage to her love of them, we even placed a fresh-picked bouquet on the altar at my mother's April funeral.

But this spring I went out to the field every few days all through late March and early April searching for the first crocuses and didn't find a single one. We'd had an unusually mild winter and then a couple of spring blizzards, so that even if the days were by then unseasonably warm, kneeling and peering into the mouth of a gopher hole on the north side of a hill—this one not freshly dug but plainly, by the fresh earth scratched up, newly in use—I saw a pad of ice before the tunnel curved out of sight in darkness. So, I thought, perhaps the ground hadn't warmed sufficiently for the first flowers to come to life.

While I was searching—on the north side of a long slope where they bloom every year—I noticed how brown the needles of the creeping juniper were, instead of green as they usually are all year round, probably also because it hadn't enough snow cover. Juniper in its various forms belongs to the cypress family, said to be the most widespread tree species in the world, varying from huge trees to the low, shrubby form (*Juniperus horizontalis*) we have in southwest Saskatchewan. Large patches of juniper, as much as twenty feet by twenty feet, grow on the steep hillsides where the ground is so eroded by drought, wind, and the action of snowpacks and water that no grass can establish a foothold. In such light brown and mini-mal amount of topsoil, the juniper takes hold and, spreading, keeps the hillside from crumbling away completely. Most local people appreciate this ecological benefit, although I've heard of one who'd like to get rid of it in the startlingly mistaken notion that it has crowded out grass that would otherwise grow there.

The juniper branches were covered with faded berries that last fall were a lovely, smoky blue. My books suggest that not so many years ago these berries wouldn't be here at all, but would have been picked by Amerindian women the previous autumn, who would have crushed them and mixed them into pemmican to give it flavour and nutrition—rich in vitamin C—or else to make a berry soup. They would have brewed the berries, too, to make a tea to aid any ailments of the stomach and digestive tract, or brewed the roots to make a liniment for muscular pain, rheumatism, and arthritis, although another source says that Amerindians brewed the berries (rather than the roots) for this purpose. The Cree, it is said, smoked the berries in pipes as a cure for asthma, while other people inhaled the fumes of the tea, or others (the Gros Ventres) drank a tea made from the berries for the same purpose. And since juniper berries contain oil, sometimes the berries were crushed and the oil rubbed on the skin to keep away insects or to give a horse's coat shine. Today juniper berries are used in medicines to promote the proper functioning of the urinary tract, and for a long time have provided the flavour in gin, but they are also an ingredient added to a number of other foods, from candy to meat products.

Once I decided to have a look at the uses Plains people put juniper to—boughs, berries, needles, roots—I laughed. To judge by my sources, everybody used various parts of it for more or less everything: to aid in childbirth and the expulsion of the afterbirth, to create a fumigant and antiseptic by burning the strongly scented boughs, to create a diuretic by chewing the berries—it was listed in medical literature in the United States for many years as such an agent—to control bleeding, to stop diarrhoea. The list goes on. Peigan women even boiled juniper berry pits till they were softened and then strung them to make necklaces.

I can never pass a patch of juniper without bending down and putting a branch to my face to inhale directly the clear piney scent that hovers in the air when you pass, or when I'm tired, I'll often find a patch of juniper to sit on. Inevitably, because it's so springy, I find myself lying back, staring up at the clouds floating by, buoyed up by this plant, feeling as if I were lying on one of the clouds themselves. When I read that Plains people used the boughs in various ways in spiritual ceremonies, I had no difficulty seeing why. Yet I don't recall reading or being told by any old people around here that perhaps at Christmas they cut the boughs and brought them in to scent the house. This was at least partly because it grows only on certain eroded, sloping hillsides and wouldn't have been available to everyone. But neither do I remember anyone born and brought up here, not even those who have the patience to pick cactus berries for jelly, who has mentioned to me picking juniper berries and using them as food.

Juniper may be prevalent, but the plant that's the icon of the West is sage, (unless it's tumbleweed, actually a number of plants, most of which aren't native but which arrived with the settlers, although a type of psoralea native to the area is tumbleweed too). Certainly I'd seen sage in the fields of my childhood, but I barely remember it, since there was so much else to look at, and we kids were always more fascinated by the forest than we were by open meadows. In southwest Saskatchewan, however, we're in the Old West of the cowboy movies of the forties and fifties, and sage is everywhere in varying degrees.

Sage is indigenous and grows naturally in a particular kind of soil which happens not to be of much use for agricultural purposes, not fertile, that is, but it is also, according to forage specialists, an "invader." Where there's overgrazing and thus a weakening of the roots of the grasses and forbs, sage is one of the plants that will move in and crowd out the weakened plants. And cattle don't like it, unless there's nothing else to eat, apparently because of its aroma as it is very high in protein. Antelope, however, winter on it.

A field so overgrazed that it's largely sage might as well be ploughed up and farmed, or else ploughed and seeded back to grass, because it appears that it won't go back to grass on its own. And wherever settlers dug barns and sheds out of hillsides, or abandoned their farms and hauled away their shacks, one or more kinds of sage is likely to be growing in the disturbed ground.

Its Latin name is *Artemisia,* named, according to the Roman writer Pliny, after a queen in Asia Minor who built one of the seven wonders of the ancient world (and the first mausoleum), the Tomb of Mausolus, for her husband around 351 B.C., at Halicarnassus, Asia Minor. Apparently the Mediterranean variety and the North American variety belong to different families, but the name travelled to the New World with the first explorers, and although Artemisia's mausoleum was destroyed by an earthquake before the fifteenth century, its builder's name still lives on in this faraway continent undiscovered in her day. And here it stands as a scourge, or as a blessing, depending on who you are.

Ranchers, for instance, don't love sage, but I do, for its strong, pleasant odour, for its colour—a sort of pale, silvered aqua in an otherwise mostly yellow-grey-tan-khaki landscape—and for the downright prettiness of the pasture and prairie sage varieties (which are herbs), although the large shrub variety, silver sagebrush, isn't so pretty, since so much of it is twisted, shredding, grey limbs. No one wants to see a field completely taken over by it. We newcomers rarely use the plant for anything more than decorative purposes, and I wondered if Amerindians had used it for anything.

I found that one of the attractive varieties, prairie sage, also known as white sage, whose Latin name is *Artemisia ludoviciana* (referring to Louisanna Territory), had many important uses among Amerindians. Chiefly, its leaves were burned as incense to drive away evil spirits, especially in purification rites, but they were also crushed for headaches, sinus attacks, and nosebleeds. According to one source, the Crow used a strong tea made of the leaves as a deodorant and antiperspirant for the underarms and feet. Other peoples made a poultice of it for sores, wounds, burns, and eczema, and used it as an inhalant for respiratory problems in a "sweat." It is also listed in all sources as a plant Amerindian women made into a tea and drank for irregular menstruation.

As for diet, I found no record of Amerindians using it as food, but it remains a plant of great importance used in sacred ceremonies in contrast to the rest of us who can't find a single use for it (it's the Mediterranean variety, *Salvia officinalis*, that is used as a cooking spice and in aromatherapy potions) and would like to reduce its presence to a bare minimum.

On a day in early April, as I sat in the field on the south side of a grassy hill, with the sun shining down on me strongly but the wind so forceful and cold that taking off my gloves to touch the plants was uncomfortable, I spotted what I thought, by its gnarled, twisted, silver-grey stem and sparse pale aqua foliage, was a silver sagebrush.

I noticed it because it was the only one in a wide area of yellow-and-cream grass and because an animal had been nibbling it and had actually dug into its roots, leaving behind a scattering of fairly large round, by this time golden-coloured pellets. I concluded the animal had to have been a jackrabbit, since we never see antelope in this field. I thought the plant was sage, but smelling it, I couldn't catch even the faintest scent, and I realized that this shrub had to be winterfat.

Humans apparently didn't use winterfat either for food or for medicine, but because it has excellent nutritious content that stays high all winter—hence the name—making it highly valued as forage for livestock, it is certainly regarded by ranchers as a precious, although too rare, plant. I'm not the only one who has trouble identifying it. Even one of the books I consulted begins its discussion of the plant by saying, "Winterfat, or white-sage ..." but giving the plant the Latin name *Eurotia lanata (Pursh),* which doesn't contain the word *artemisia,* while everyone else identifies white sage as a type of artemisia.

Or does this matter? After all, it is scientists—botanists—who decided what these plants would be called, using their own system of discrimination, a very different one than that used by aboriginal people around the world. Lévi-Strauss, in his book *The Savage Mind,* comments especially on the potent interest of aboriginal people in all aspects of the world in which they live, especially in its plants, about which their traditional knowledge and finely discriminating systems of classification are nothing short of amazing. Nor is their system based solely on use, according to Lévi-Strauss, as botanists once claimed, in so doing disparaging the intelligence of First Peoples everywhere. Science provides a different classificatory system for which it claims the only truth, or at least the primary truth, an arrogance I've always found shocking.

And who gave it that odd but charming name of winterfat? Could it have been Amerindians, since it is a native plant, not an introduced one? I can't find it in the *Oxford English Dictionary,* and none of my plant books explain where the name came from. I begin to suspect that it's a translation of a Cree, Siksika, or Nakota name.

Reading Felipe Fernandez-Armesto's *Truth,* I am glad to discover that the old idea that aboriginal people were like children in their thinking and that their societies failed to mature as European civilization had done has been discredited. Today, scholars easily point out the complexity and profundity of the traditional ideas about life and the world of such peoples everywhere. Their ideas, their systems of thought, were merely vastly different from European thought and stemmed from observations of and intense experience with the natural world, all of which Europeans had long since forgotten. They were not "primitive" or "savage" or wrong in their explanations of the world. They were different.

Although I hadn't the slightest notion that such a truth would ever be of any importance to me, my travels in the field were leading somewhere, though to a destination I'd never imagined.

Wandering the field one afternoon in early May, I found the ground studded in patches with tiny white flowers, so abundant that from a distance they might have been mistaken for thin drifts of snow. I got down on my knees and saw it was something my book tells me is called moss phlox, or *Phlox hoodii* Richardson (named after the midshipman on the Sir John Franklin Expedition to the Arctic of 1819–22). Each plant is dark green, looks like a clump of moss, and is covered with small white blossoms. The biggest of these five-petalled flowers might be slightly more than a half-inch across; the whole plant isn't more than two inches above the ground at its highest, and when it's not in flower, nobody but a botanist would notice it at all. One of my books claims it's called "Mayflower," but I've never heard anyone call it that. Apparently it's a herb, not a true moss, and after flowering, it forms a big part of the ground cover in the field.

We'd just had a much-needed inch of rain, and things were popping up all over, and as I knelt and parted the dead grass and new green sprouts with my fingers to see what I could see, I came across some yellow flowers blooming against a cream-and-gold rock, smaller than my smallest fingernail, on a plant that wasn't two inches high. I recognized the flowers at once as violets, Nuttall's yellow violets to be exact. I couldn't get over the plant's minuteness, how delicate and lovely it was, although from looking at the pictures alone in the plant guides, you'd never guess how tiny the actual plant is. But such is the nature of much of the plant life of this field. To fully appreciate it, I was beginning to find, you have to study it with your nose only a couple of inches from it. Then a whole new universe of beauty opens to the jaded or the skeptical eye, and a field that at first glance appears to be boring and barren turns out to be filled with treasures every bit as gorgeous as the tropical blooms of Hawaii or Mexico.

True, I'd never seen a field like this one anywhere else I'd lived in Saskatchewan. Though it's easy to dismiss this observation by saying it's the prickly pear cactus and sage that make the field so different, its uniqueness, I was learning, comes from a number of other indigenous plants, all of which don't exist or else don't combine in quite the same way anywhere else in the province.

Unlike the rest of the province, this is not a green landscape—only for a while in spring, and only if we aren't in the middle of one of our characteristic, severe drought cycles. Mostly we have that first flush of the green of new growth in the spring, but by mid-July in the intense heat and with lack of precipitation—recently it was over a year between significant rainfalls, and we'd had very little snow— the range grasses have cured on the stem and are a pale gold. Driving down the road or riding across the prairie, you're surrounded by the long, wide fields of pale yellow, cream, or tawny gold, and the sunset's long, low rays turn the pale fields and hills pink and rose, apricot and gold. In late fall and winter, the fields turn grey, charcoal, dun, and everyone prays for snow just to brighten the drabness.

But flashes of bright colour are out there. Often when I'm walking, I'll spot a bit of red in the middle of a distant stand of grass, and thinking I've found some rare, bright flower, I've gone there eagerly, parted the grass, and found instead a patch of red lichen on a rock. Lichen is another of the plants that make for the unique character of this field.

Some areas of the field have a bountiful supply that is pale green and delicately multiple-branched—a piece of it looks like a diagram of the inside of the human lungs—and lies unattached, loosely on the ground or on a rock. I have a small piece of it on one of my shelves, and it looks identical today to the way it was the day I picked it up, presumably because lichen is the product of the symbiotic relationship of an alga and a fungus and is only sometimes rooted to the ground or a tree. A book on lichens informs me this one is called *Xanthoparmelia chlorochroa*, a term I find awkward in everyday use but, since it doesn't seem to have a common name, will have to do.

I find no record of lichen used as food or medicine on the northern Great Plains (although Icelanders make soup of one kind), but without it, the fields would be uniformly green or gold or dun, as it covers rocks in a variety of bright or pale colours, the brightest being the red or orange or rust that so often fools me. But it also occurs in shades of green, from pale to a rare, brilliant lime, and in gold, yellow, black, grey, cream, and white that delight the eye.

Whenever I walk in the field, the moment that gives me the most pleasure is when I come upon an area of very short, curly, grey-coloured grass. In these patches the grass doesn't rise much more than an inch above the ground, and instead of the individual blades sticking straight up, they are horizontal to the ground and curved into roughly a semicircle. (They're only a couple of inches long and very narrow.) This is what the people of the area call "buffalo grass," and any attentive visitor, not having seen it before, notices these patches at once and asks what they are. Examining a patch closely in early spring, I thought this grass was merely shoots from the club moss that covered the ground below it, but careful looking showed that it was a separate plant growing up through the club moss.

When it's fully grown, the blades are not taller than fifty centimetres, or about eighteen inches, but it's easily recognizable by its heads, which a woman once said to me always reminded her of little eyelashes—curved and brushy on one side only. Ranchers like this grass a lot for its nutrition as forage and for its hardiness in the driest places, and one of my books tells me that some Amerindians used it to predict the winter by counting the number of seed stalks—one meaning a mild winter, and several indicating a greater degree of severity.

Since settlement, the people of this area have referred to the native prairie as shortgrass prairie. Botanists insist it's properly called "mixed-grass" prairie, and no amount of argument will make them change their minds. My objection to this is that the term "shortgrass" was popular parlance (according to the OED, first used in *Harper's* magazine in 1883) for a native range where the grass was shorter than it is in areas which get more rainfall. The point being that "shortgrass" is not a scientific term but one which was taken over by scientists and redefined by them, a mistake of diplomacy on their part, creating a permanent grouchiness between the two sectors, as local people rather resent their language being abitrarily redefined by others.

Buffalo grass, or blue grama (*Bouteloua gracilis*), the one I've just described, is one of the main grasses of true shortgrass prairie, but it grows in abundance in mixed-grass prairie too. Our specialists insist that true buffalo grass doesn't grow in Saskatchewan, that the plant everyone around here has always called buffalo grass is really a "third cousin" to the real thing—*Buchloë dactyloides*—which grows in Montana, Colorado, and Wyoming to the south. That to the naked eye it appears to be the same plant, albeit a little shorter and with fewer stalks (due, we think, to the dryness of this region), is of no account to the botanists. I think that in pioneer days Saskatchewan people began to call that grass "buffalo grass" because so many of the original settlers had come up from the western United States, bringing their nomenclature for such similar-appearing plants with them.

Walking across much of this prairie, our feet make a delicious crunching noise instead of the silky swish of grass in regions of greater precipitation. Our buffalo grass is partly responsible for the crunch, but even more so, it is caused by club moss (*Prairie selaginella*). Everywhere here it forms a mat under and around the other plants or else exists by itself on open, dry spots, and it is said to be one of the commonest mosses in a very dry area like this one.

There are lots of varieties of club moss, but this is the only one listed as occurring in this area of Saskatchewan, and surprisingly, I find it's classified as a fern and a forb and not as a moss at all. It, too, is greatly valued by those who understand its function as a plant that helps stop the bad effects of erosion, a constant problem in an arid countryside, where if plants die as a result of drought—and they do all the time, even cactus—and nothing is left to hold the soil in place, the steady winds blow it away.

Forage specialists whose not ignoble job it is to find ways to enhance forage opportunities for ranchers' cattle, have suggested something called "range renovation," which is to go over the prairie with spikes and poke holes in it to break this cover, the theory being that the plant stops moisture from breaking through to the soil below and thus prevents grass from growing. (And club moss is of no use as forage for cattle and horses.) But in one study I found where range renovation was applied, the results were reported as mixed, the worst being a decrease in blue grama grass—the valuable plant we call buffalo grass.

The Amerindian people, who made their lives wholly on and from and through the land, however, apparently didn't worry about club moss. It is thought to have been brewed by the Siksika as a medicinal tea for women (presumably having to do with menstruation), and for colds, sore throats, tuberculosis, flu, and "chest problems." It is listed, too, as a food harvested in summer by the Peigan of the Blackfoot Confederacy, although not all elders agree about this. If it was used, it appears it was dried as a spice for meat.

Often I've remarked on the wide fields of native grass I've ridden horses on or walked through. That was a sufficient description for my purposes and, in fact, when you drive past them, that is what they appear to be. But this observation is true only where there is a good supply of moisture, and not always even then. Although the vast prairie region extending down into the United States and north of here at least a couple of hundred miles grows something like 140 species of grass (the other components listed above bringing the total number of possible species to around 200), the view from a distance is nonetheless one of a uniform grassy cover.

The field of this book also appears from the distance to be simply grass with rocks protruding here and there, but as I've indicated, as soon as you enter and walk in it, you find that a fair amount of the growth isn't grass at all, but cactus, forbs, sedges, and shrubs. Not to mention the areas of rocks, the burn-outs and blow-outs, the saline flats and the hardpan, and more rarely, in isolated areas, hoodoos, which are hills decimated of all plants by drought and sometimes also by overgrazing, so that wind and water action has eroded them into the eerie shapes familiar in Western movies.

In an area as dry as this one, which includes poor-quality brown soils, and sparse winter snow despite the degree of cold that people from warmer climates can't even imagine, what we call abundance bears no resemblance to anything but an Inuit's or an Icelander's idea of abundance. Or perhaps that of an Amerindian living here before the settlers came.

Generally, we think of abundance (if you raise livestock and not wheat) as long, wide fields of thick, tall grass. Our grass is eighteen to twenty-four inches high at its tallest—in contrast to "tall grass" prairie, where the grass is five or six or more feet high. The only natural remnant of this prairie in Canada is a small area within the city of Winnipeg, the rest having been ploughed for farming or razed to build cities and towns. The dividing line between the two kinds of prairie is Wallace Stegner's hundredth meridian (roughly at Winnipeg), to the west of which precipitation drops drastically, and which he used as the boundary line of the beginning of the true West. We are in the driest area of the dry side of that boundary, hence our scaled-down idea of abundance.

Of course, as I've said, there are stretches of indigenous grass in the field, uninterrupted by other kinds of plants: June grass, needle-and-thread or spear grass, northern and western wheatgrass, various blue grasses, and fescues, as well as some I can't identify. The great variety of grasses, which grow in patches of single kinds rather than intermingling, are constantly fascinating to watch as they grow through their cycles.

But an introduced grass called crested wheatgrass is invading up the draws more and more every year, crowding out the native grasses and killing them off. When I complained of this to a prominent botanical expert at a conference in Regina, he looked at me pityingly and said that this was of no account, since it was all forage—"Wasn't it, dear?" Chastised and astonished, having thought I was talking to a prairie lover, I didn't say a word in reply. In retrospect, I think I should have just kicked him in the shins. It may not have explained anything to him, but I would have felt better.

Crested wheatgrass was brought to Canada from Siberia in 1915. For years it was seen as better forage than native plants, and acres and acres of native grasses were ploughed up and seeded with this introduced species at the behest of crop and forage scientists working in agricultural research stations and at universities. Lots of ranchers were converted to this doctrine and ploughed up their prairie to seed it, too. It even happened on the Butala ranch, to put back to grass areas which had been originally ploughed by the first, long-gone, homesteaders, because native grass seed was at the time virtually impossible to obtain and, when it was, prohibitively expensive. Now we find crested wheatgrass invading everywhere, and nobody can think of a way to stop it that won't damage other life forms to an unacceptable degree.

Its chief merit is obviously its hardiness. But it's barely hardier than native prairie—we see indigenous plants invading the crested wheatgrass in our yard now—and native prairie, as I hope I've demonstrated, has a good many other qualities, the greatest being its tremendous biodiversity, which is utterly lacking in a monocrop of crested wheatgrass. Nor is native prairie so unpleasant to look at or to walk through because of its stiffness and dryness, both attributes the single-minded search for forage for imported livestock doesn't care about. Crested wheatgrass also mines the soil of its nutrients, especially nitrogen, while in the native plant populations there are plants that put back nitrogen in their own time frame. Not only is it a very hard user of the nutrients in the soil, it doesn't return anything to speak of, and isn't even sod-forming, because it's a bunchgrass; that is, it grows in clumps rather than as a mat of single plants as lawn grass does.

And yet, despite our dislike of the plant and the fact we didn't seed it, or our great desire to keep that field intact as an example of true native prairie in top-notch condition, we have to watch helplessly as crested wheatgrass invades farther and farther every year, killing off the native plants and changing utterly the character and potential uses of the field. No more Indian breadroot, no more berries, no more juniper or sage or winterfat or moss phlox or true mosses or penstemon, gumbo evening primroses, yellow violets, scarlet mallow, prairie everlasting, death camas or wild onion or the half-dozen kinds of vetches, no more lichens, no more buffalo grass—no more shortgrass prairie.

Eventually this spring we found crocuses, although it was late April to early May before they finally appeared, dotting the hillsides with their fuzzy, silver-grey stems and leaves and their mauve-to-purple, yellow-centred flowers. I sighed with relief when at last they came, and thought ahead to the long seasons when I'd walk and think or, rather, not-think, but lose myself instead in discovering and studying the seemingly endless, precious bounty of the field.

Devotion, I thought to myself, that is the word to describe how I feel now about the field: I have given myself over to it, and it rewards me every trip I make out to it by showing me something new, something surprising, something beautiful. This seemed to me reward enough for conquering the bewildering tiredness I had to overcome, some days with every step, to get there, or for the work I left undone at home, or for the hot sun or the wind or the insects I had to endure. Every time I went there, I was rewarded for my growing reverence, my *devotion*, by the peace that crept over me while I was in the field and by the quiet happiness it gave to me.

One day after I had left it and was walking down a trail beyond it towards home, I stopped dead in my tracks, because directly in front of my toes, emerging out of the hard-packed earth where nothing else was growing, was a plant five or six inches tall and so pristine that it looked as if it had just broken through the ground into the light and air. As I stared at it, I saw it had a kind of hyperreality; it virtually glistened with it. The plant was in flower and unmarred by a single blemish or smudge or malformed part. The other plants lining the path looked drab and ordinary beside it.

It was so perfect, so precise, that to my eyes it looked as if it had just sprung up there by the flick of an enchanter's wand. And I knew at once without the slightest doubt, despite still not having looked it up, that this was Indian breadroot.

Chapter 3

VISIONS

A NEIGHBOUR REMARKED TO ME THAT SHE HAD ONCE seen a very big white coyote watering down at the river, his coat gleaming silver in the moonlight. I said, "You know, that sounds like a dream," just as she said, sounding a little surprised herself, "But maybe it was a dream."

In the ordinary, everyday world, a white coyote would be so rare as to be almost unprecedented. The person who saw it would rush for a camera and shout for other family members to come and see it too; she wouldn't merely stand serenely, filled with wonder, watching it. So I suspect that it was a dream, except that all of us know that sometimes when we're asleep and dreaming, what happens there is so marvellous that we are never quite sure that we were asleep, but feel that in some inexplicable way we had entered another, unknown world, a mythical world of great beauty where everything is imbued with intense and powerful meaning, if only we could decipher it, a world where silver-white coyotes, their coats gleaming in the bright light of the moon, exist and go about their business and communicate with humans, with the dreamers, without speaking.

This is the world of visions. In order to make it acceptable for the intelligent, educated late-twentieth-century individual steeped in the scientific attitude to talk about it, psychologists demythologize this age-old human experience by calling it an "altered state of consciousness." Having had a few of them myself, I prefer to call such experiences what they are—visions—and to describe them privately, collectively, as mystical experiences. And if it is possible, as it is, to enter that world through a door in sleep into something we call a dream, it is equally possible, although perhaps less common, to enter that world when one is wide awake.

The reader will hear echoes of the work of Joseph Campbell and of Carl Jung in these ideas—both of whom were concerned with the world of mythology as it relates to the human psyche and, of course, to dreams and their meanings and relationship to the mythological world. In the end, though, I think all of this is about the divine in the sense of the supernatural, the spiritual, an unseen power or powers. And it strikes me as very sad that in our efforts to pull ourselves up out of the quagmire of superstition, we have also (mostly by simple denial, or by attempts to explain it away) tried to remove ourselves from the visionary world and the visionary experience.

As I've grown older, I have had such experiences more often, and more often when I'm wide awake. I can never predict when I'll have them or think of any good reason why, or always recognize I'm having one while it is happening but like my neighbour, recognize it for what it was only afterward. While it's happening, it is so compelling, so all-encompassing that there can be no questioning, no bewilderment, no doubt.

Sometimes my experiences have fit William James's requirements for genuine mystical experience—as ineffable, transient, having a knowledge component, and occurring in the passivity of the subject—but just as often they don't have all four components. If I were being a purist, I'd find it necessary to separate meticulously one experience from another, create categories for them, and give each category a name. I haven't enough of them; sometimes I think each one belongs to its own category. Thus, the various names already existing in the vernacular: experiences that are clairvoyant, mediumistic, telepathic, telekinetic, spiritual, and so on. They just happen, and while they are all valuable in their own ways, they have in common their capacity to surprise, to create change in the subject, and to offer a sense of revelation. Although it occurs to me to wonder if this last may be only our inexperience with them.

The earliest experience of this sort I can clearly remember occurred when I was eight or nine years old and making my First Communion in the Catholic church, when it seemed to me that what I had been told to call the Holy Ghost came down and lit in my chest, and although I had others in the years between then and my removal to this place to live, in the last ten or so years they seem to be increasing. I recently read a paper, part of her work for her doctorate, by a Unitarian clergywoman who studied the frequency of what we call "mystical experiences" among members of Unitarian congregations and clergy, examining her sample by both gender and age. She reports that of all categories and both genders, women between the ages of fifty-one and sixty-five had the highest frequency of "felt presence, voice, and vision" experiences and were also, of those who had them, the least frightened of them. Tentatively, she suggests this result might be because older women have "softer boundaries" than either younger women or men or the elderly. It is a provocative study and led me immediately to think of all the women burned as witches—often reported to have been ordinary housewives—and to my own increasing number of experiences, which it helps to make less extraordinary, more in the natural order of things.

Sometimes I don't know what to call these visions. A few years ago my husband and I went on a yachting trip—a seventy-one-foot boat under sail called *Darwin Sound*—around Orkney and the Shetland Islands north of mainland Scotland. One of the islands we visited was Fair Isle, the island in the North Sea only three miles long and a mile and a half wide, famous for its hand-knit wool sweaters of most intricate and distinctive design. The "Fair" in Fair Isle is thought to be Old Norse and probably means "far" or "far island." It is a very isolated place with a population of perhaps sixty-five people, serviced by a small ferry—which looked like a fishing boat to me—and by small plane. Part of it is also a national bird sanctuary.

Docked behind us at the wharf was the ferry, and next to us another sailboat somewhat smaller than ours, all stained wood (our captain said it was a classic type of Danish boat), and another yacht under sail full of a large number of unshaven, bulky-looking German men who appeared to be businessmen on an adventure. (I said good evening to them—it seemed the only polite thing to do—and instead of receiving back perhaps one mumbled "Hi" or surly "Evening," as I expected, got back a loud, polite "Good Evening," simultaneously from them. The number seventeen sticks in my mind. It was quite startling, not to mention embarrassing, and I wished I hadn't spoken.)

I found the island, as we approached it finally after five hours of sailing across empty waters, to have a kind of dark, brooding presence as it appeared on the horizon and grew larger and larger—its wind-and-water-sculptured high green cliffs, its loneliness, or something else, some ambience that I couldn't put my finger on. Perhaps it was only the light, of a kind I'm not used to, lacking the brilliant clarity of the light of the landlocked Great Plains of North America. Even now, staring at my snapshots, I can see it. I found it one of the most powerful and singular places I've ever visited and was drawn to it immediately, although, as far as I know, this wasn't true of others on our boat who seemed to gaze at the island in a speculative, tentative fashion, with interest, but less than great enthusiasm.

It was late in the day when we arrived, so all we did that I can recall was go birdwatching. (Here I saw puffins for the first time.) The next day we visited the home of one of the Fair Isle knitters, a co-operative, I believe, and our fellow guests ordered sweaters, we walked the island, had small adventures each of our own kind, and ended back on our boat having dinner together that evening. But something drew me outside, some inarticulate need to experience more of this place, some yearning as if there were more experience to be had before I could leave contented. When we'd finished eating, I put on my jacket and left the boat by myself to go walking. One field in particular, near the wharf, appealed to me, and since I hadn't had a chance that day to go there, now I set out.

Fair Isle is just below sixty degrees north latitude and this was June, so even though it was perhaps ten o'clock at night, we were just entering twilight. I was walking carefully, staying alert because there were sheep in the field, and as it was spring I was afraid there might be a nasty-tempered ram, and certain large birds about had the unpleasant habit, we'd discovered, of dive-bombing people. As a country girl alert to such accidents, I wasn't too keen to step into any fresh sheep droppings, either. I remember that late evening as having a kind of luminescence to it, a kind of resonance—the moist air, the rich colour of the waning light, the hypergreen of the well-cropped, grass-covered fields.

I walked slowly, carefully, heading towards the green top of the highest cliff on the island. At one point, glancing down, I saw a grass-covered round lump in front of my feet, about eight inches in circumference and six or so inches tall at its highest point. I made out at once that it was a grass-covered stone. As I was about to go around it, I noticed that there was another, identical to the first, to its left and also one to its right. I kept turning and as I turned I saw more stones. I saw that I was standing in the exact centre of a grass-covered, perfectly symmetrical stone circle.

I stared down at it, turning. At this point I knew little about Celts (although possibly by then I was beginning to figure out that I may be one—Irish-Scots on my mother's side, and on my father's, with Acadian ancestors from France in the seventeenth century, most likely in the beginning also Celt), and I couldn't figure out what to make of a stone circle here, in this place. On our travels already we'd seen the massive stone circles of the Ring of Brogdar on Orkney and also the nearby Standing Stones of Stenness whose origins, though unknown, are Stone Age, long before the arrival of the Vikings. But this circle was rather more like a small tepee ring, and I couldn't recall having heard that the Norse had made stone circles.

I thought in surprise and bewilderment and, ultimately, disbelief, *this can't be!* and I stepped out of the stone circle and went on my way. But not far, for I no longer felt like trying to reach the top of the cliff. I turned and went back to the boat (and all the scruffy-looking German men said in unison, "Good Evening," to me). I told my fellow travellers what I'd seen, and there was some desultory conversation about it. Someone remarked, I recall, that he didn't think there was a people who hadn't at some point in its history made stone circles. I don't know if this is true or not.

The next morning after breakfast, as we were preparing to set sail for the Shetland Islands, I made a quick trip, again alone, back to the field to take a look in full daylight at the stone circle. To my astonishment, nothing looked the same about the field; I couldn't recognize it as the field I'd seen the night before; I couldn't find the spot where I'd stood and looked down; there was no grass-covered, perfect stone circle anywhere in the field, only sheep droppings and overgrazed, inch-high bright green grass. The field looked so different in daylight that I saw at once it was pointless to keep searching.

Plainly, I had been "taken over," had entered an altered state of consciousness, had had a vision of that stone circle which, when I was having it, I was completely unaware of. I've no idea why; I've no idea if it was "given" to me, by whom or what, or if it merely hovered there all the time, waiting for someone open enough to walk into it. Or was it that I'd stepped into a pocket of time from another era? And if so, how did I do that? Why can't I do it whenever I feel like it? Why did I fail to recognize the experience for what it was when it was happening? Or perhaps the stone circle was really there, but buried feet or yards under the grass, waiting for an archeologist to dig it up. If so, then I could call the experience "clairvoyance," couldn't I?

I can give you the exact date of another vision: It was June 3, 1998. I was driving down the highway from Eastend to a larger town called Shaunavon twenty miles down the road. I name these towns because they exist in the world, they are on maps, people you can visit or call on the telephone live in them. The highway is narrow but asphalt-covered, it has a moderate amount of traffic, people have died in traffic accidents on it. It is a very real, if remote and obscure, road only about thirty miles from the Montana border and running parallel to it. The little town of Eastend sits in a deep valley, hills rise up around it, a narrow river winds its way through it, and grain elevators, the old-fashioned wooden ones that are so rapidly disappearing, rise above the trees.

The highway out of the town heading east runs up a high hill before it flattens out and, curving, runs on east to Shaunavon. Over the driver's left shoulder Chimney Coulee rises above the landscape to a peak at Anxiety Butte, forming the extreme east end of the Cypress Hills on which not one cypress grows but, instead, lodgepole pines. On the driver's right, south, the land rolls away, descending, to the United States, and our small river flows down, into the Missouri. There used to be patches of grassland along that highway, but nowadays it is nearly all ploughed and seeded to crops, and above the fields, to the left and right and straight ahead, the windshield is filled with nothing but sky.

I had spent most of the winter of 1998 in the city looking after an invalid sister dying of breast cancer, not diagnosed until it had become lung cancer and, save a miracle, there would be no cure. I was home for a few days and, for some prosaic reason like bill-paying or grocery shopping, was for the thousandth time making that drive from Eastend to Shaunavon. I was tired, I was relaxed—my sister was in good hands and was, for the moment, stable and not in pain—I had a few blessed days at home and was savouring every moment of them. I climbed the curving hill at the end of the valley, coming up out of Eastend in my 1996 Chevy Blazer, a real vehicle, painted the blue of the sky with silver trim. I let up on the gas since nobody else was on the road, and for once—someone else was worrying abut medication, oxygen, symptoms, meals to tempt an invalid, the suffering in her face and eyes—I didn't feel rushed. I needed to slow down, to take it easy, to just drive and not think.

That day the view through the windshield was of low, fat clouds, blue and mauve-tinted, with rounded, charcoal bottoms. There was a wind blowing across the highway from north to south, and it might soon begin to rain. I saw all this, felt it, did not think about it. I was for the moment a creature of the road and of the landscape; it was there and so was I. An antelope came up out of the ditch on my left and I braked. I'd only been going about fifty miles per hour, thinking, there he is again, I wonder where his partner is; he crossed the road on an angle in front of me, moving fast as antelope do, and —how beautiful antelope are—I watched him run down into the ditch on the other side and up onto the farmland where he stopped, turned, and faced me, waiting. As he ran down into the ditch, I saw first his white rump and then the wind rippling his short black mane, and a small delight grew in me, low in my abdomen.

I pushed on the gas and drove on, perhaps ten feet, when suddenly a shock went through me. *What was that?* I rehearsed what I had just seen: how the clouds had parted narrowly and beams of white light shone down on the road in front of me and the antelope, how his body turned slightly away from me, his head lifted, and a wide beam of bluish white light bathed him, in it his warm-brown body turned a hazy blue-white and—*he became a unicorn.*

I think I laughed. I drove on, my whole viscera open, in awe, in amazement, in joy. My chest did something funny, I'm not sure what. It opened up; it melded into my breath. I think, for some minuscule portion of time, I thought I could fly. But I didn't, I drove on to Shaunavon. And I didn't tell anyone. Not for months. But I did not—I do not—doubt what I saw. And I knew, too, not that I understood then or that I understand even now, that what had happened was that my eyes had opened to see *what is always there.*

In that instant the "real" world had cracked and split narrowly apart— "a veil shimmered apart and there he was in another light, white world," my journal says—and I was allowed a glimpse of the mythic world we're told exists right beside or behind, or maybe inside, the "real" one of Chevy Blazers and hard-topped black roads, and death, and cans of peaches and corn in the Shaunavon Co-op.

Driving across land only three or four miles from where certain Plains people had once sought visions too—according to the stories, apparently of things like indigenous animals that would communicate with them—I saw a unicorn. Astounding as it was, and beautiful, that it was a unicorn I saw struck me as simply bizarre, for what have unicorns to do with North America? What, especially, with the Great Plains? I am not one of those people who are charmed by the figure of the unicorn and fill their houses with everything from unicorn-shaped pillows and glass sculptures of unicorns to posters of them. I've never considered them as anything but mythical creatures in the same class as mermaids and seven-headed dragons.

Cirlot writes of the surprising universality of the symbol of the unicorn, pointing out that it occurs even in the Vedas, which are dated at 1500 to 500 B.C. Unicorns are mentioned in the Old Testament, in Job 39:9. Robert Graves reports that the British author Charles Doughty (1843–1926), in his *Travels in Arabia Deserta*, says that the unicorn must be "a large, very dangerous antelope called *wothyi* or 'wild ox' by the Arabs." That an antelope should actually be a unicorn seemed fitting to me in a physical sense—that sleek, trim, precise, muscled-yet-slender body, its daintiness, not shaggy like a bison or lumbering like a bear or too rapid like a weasel, and its simple perfection of form. But I did not think that there were unicorns hiding behind the veil of daily life in North America too.

I'm not afraid of these experiences, I never have been. My

strongest emotion is wonder, followed by gratitude, and then the years of mulling them over to try to make them fit somehow into my life, as having meaning for it, as being *directed* to it. And the vast and unending puzzlement about the world they reveal. Is it real? Might I live in it? Would I want to if I could ever see enough of it to understand it in some coherence? Does it have coherence? Is it where I will go when I die? Or is it only experience to be likened to the flashes of light that emit from a faceted jewel as it turns in a jeweller's fingers?

Our culture runs in terror from such experiences—Hildegard of Bingen and St. Teresa of Avila notwithstanding, women who existed so long ago they can be safely discussed aloud—and allows virtually no official mention of them, except for the psychologist's "altered states of consciousness" and other pseudoscientific explanations. Those few in the world of popular culture who do allow them, do so only within a framework of exalted, God-given experience, always confirming what the recipient already knew anyway, that he/she belongs to the chosen people to whom God speaks directly. Or else immediately tries to use them to amplify personal power as in witchcraft or certain "New Age" fantasies. All of this I find frightening. But I am also sure that there are many others like me who, knowing they'll be discredited if they mention such experiences, have them but remain silent about them.

But not all cultures around the world shut out such experience from public discourse. There remain still those cultures that accept completely, and apparently in a fairly matter-of-fact way, that such experiences are part of what it is to be a human being living on this earth, and that, further, as a part of creation, they are instructive and that one is meant to act on their content. The Amerindian people of the Great Plains of North America are among those who've traditionally held this worldview.

In these cultures men sought visions in a ritualized manner by deliberately taking part in the ritual of vision questing. It is said that the purpose of the vision quest was to seek personal power, not to wield over other people but to aid in the individual's inevitably difficult passage through life, to help the individual to behave well and rightly, and to show the quester how to help his/her people.

To this end, the literature of ethnology, anthropology, and archeology tells us, young boys were taken by elders to lonely sites and, with appropriate prayers and offerings, stripped usually of all or nearly all clothing and were left alone to fast for several days and to seek a vision. Such a vision might be called a "dream," or a "dream-vision." Accounts of these experiences use all these names, and there seems to be no particular distinction among ways of fulfilling the quest, although the dreams of certain great dreamers, such as Black Elk or Fools Crow, are told and retold.

Apparently, the youth hoped to be given a spirit helper, perhaps in the form of an animal, but not always, who would give him instructions on how to stay always in the helper's good graces and offer appropriate songs, prayers, and rituals to use in order to contact the helper in the future. Quests were not always successful, or the dream given might not be considered to be sacred, and the quest might be repeated later, but if it was successful, the dreamer would usually then tell his dream to the elders and give a demonstration of the personal power he had thus acquired. Account after account (or story after story) tells of an object brought to the dreamer by the spirits during the experience, which he holds when he comes out of the dream and the spirit helpers have gone. He keeps this object always as one in which the power of his dream resides.

Adolescent girls occasionally had ritual vision quests, but it seems to be more usual that women had spontaneous visions and dreams, which, if sacred and powerful, were honoured equally with the men's. At other times in the individual's life, it appears, sometimes during a personal crisis or a major disturbance of the social order, an older person might go on another ritual vision quest to seek instruction and help from the powers of the dream-world.

In *The Perfection of the Morning*, I recounted how one day I went to a high point in the field and stood in the centre of a very small ring, and then was driven out of the circle, an inner voice—a "voiceless voice"—telling me, *You are not worthy*. As I looked back to the circle, I saw a shaman standing in it, arms raised. Yet the shaman I saw was not precisely out there, but seemed to be less in my "mind's eye" than in the centre of my forehead, where esoteric tradition places the "third eye." After that experience, I concluded that the spot had to be treated with due reverence, because surely it was, or had been, sacred. Or perhaps it's more accurate to say that I then knew this place held power.

A visitor to the field with me remarked that the site, located on the opposite side of the field from the narrow plateau that held the large circle I liked to think of as the burial tent of a Siksika chief, was perfect for vision-questing. It was isolated, high, with a long view in three directions out over the distant hills and valleys. He suggested that perhaps that was how it had been used, as there was room for only one person in the stone circle to sit, stand, or lie in a curled position.

I spoke also in that book, relative to that experience, of an account Jung gave in *Memories, Dreams, Reflections* about visiting a church in Ravenna and seeing wonderful stained-glass windows which he found out later had been destroyed in a fire centuries before. I felt that perhaps my seeing the shaman was, as with the stone circle in the sheep field on Fair Isle, an instance of the same kind of "warping" of time. Or else a vision.

It was in this field, too, that I'd found and then lost again the white dolomite sphere and cylinder. On another occasion, in a far corner of the field where I almost never go, I came upon a large chert rock, thigh-high, and maybe thirty inches in diameter. It looked as if someone had taken an axe and split off vertical slabs or chunks, any number of which lie about on the hillsides, although none of them was lying around at the foot of the rock as happens with rocks that split and crumble with age and the extreme heating and cooling through the seasons.

I considered the rock, walking around and around it, studying it, running my fingers down its angles and pressing my palms against its flatness. Then I realized that I had found a source for tool-making, that is, a rock with the right hardness and cleavage characteristics that made it suitable for tools and weapons. Amerindians must have used it, coming back to it over and over again to break off pieces. I was delighted with myself. I had found evidence of an encampment nearby and signs that women had stayed long enough to prepare hides, so it seemed reasonable that the men would have searched for a source of materials for their tools and weapons. And also, it seemed to me unlikely that horseless, nomadic people, in a country full of stones, would have carried any but perhaps their favourite small stone tools with them, but more likely that at each new campsite they might seek out rocks of the right material.

But, as with the sphere and the cylinder, when I went back months later, at first I couldn't find the stone at all, and when I finally concluded that a certain rock must have been the one I'd seen, it was no longer at all obvious what it had been used for. I had to study it carefully, dubiously. What had happened to the clean, sharp lines I'd seen where pieces had been so decisively split off? Now it was covered here and there with patches of lichen, rough-edged and ancient-looking. I couldn't tell if once again I'd been carried away to another realm of time to view it, or if I'd been given a glimpse of it as it once would have been, or if I'd simply cleaned it up in my imagination after I left it the first time, in the way that researchers have shown that witnesses of car accidents tend to amplify the noise and the damage in reporting. I simply didn't know.

I think I could have wept for the craziness of the whole business. I was as sane as the next person, I hadn't been drinking, I don't do drugs, rarely take anything more than aspirin or an antihistamine, am not a religious fanatic, don't starve myself, am in good health— and yet these *things* kept happening to me in the field. What could I do but, in frustration at my inability to find explanations and uncertainty and puzzlement as to their source and purpose, eventually shrug my shoulders and walk away?

I can't even say that I felt especially singled out by whatever was showing me these things. No one else had spent as much time in the field as I had, certainly not over the twenty-or-more years I'd been walking the field and studying what I found there. Nor had anyone else established a spiritual connection with whatever power or force or presence seemed to dwell there, for not every out-of-the-ordinary experience I had in the field had to do with archeological finds. Some of them seemed to me more clearly of a spiritual nature.

Once, walking the field in sorrow over a quarrel with a friend and speaking to the friend in my mind, rehearsing my case mentally and growing more and more anguished over it all, I suddenly felt there was someone behind me, and turned, and there was the friend, holding out a hand to me in heartfelt supplication, a phantom that, to my shame, I rejected, and that disappeared almost at once. Yet, this phantom, too, appeared more in my forehead than actually out there in the world. But on this occasion I didn't fight the apparition as I did with the stone circle on Fair Isle, and I let it appear shimmering in the centre of the patch of hardpan I'd been crossing. I knew all along that, as with the shaman, I might have forced what I saw to stay hovering there half in and half out of my mind's eye. But most assuredly this was not the same experience as imagining the friend standing there. This figure I did not conjure up myself; it simply appeared there, as if in response to the extremity of our mutual emotion carried between us over the miles.

I've said that I'd begun to use the field as other people use their churches, as a place to go when troubled, a peaceful, quiet place with an aura of the sacred about it. On another day I'd gone there because I was deeply unhappy, not over any particular thing, but just in that way we all sometimes feel, that life is too hard, that there aren't enough good things in it to compensate for all the bad. As I walked among the rocks and the grass, that gentle anguish simmered through my body, for which there seemed no cure. I moved slowly, ruminating on my misery as I went. Suddenly the voiceless voice spoke in my head: *This, too, is illusion.*

I halted, too surprised by the message to wonder then about its source. Illusion? I asked myself, and lifted my head and looked around. The sun was shining, a light breeze was blowing as it often does, the grass was still green, and the rocks with their patches of bright or pale lichen were as beautiful as they'd ever been. I was physically fine—no wounds, no illness. No one I loved was in any more trouble than he or she had been yesterday. Life was not any different today than it had been yesterday, or the day before that, or likely would be tomorrow.

Then I realized that in the moment of hearing the "voiceless voice" and then looking around, the anguish that had run through my entire body had gone, and things were once again merely what they were. I thought of how all the years since I'd become an adult I'd felt that pain, sometimes for days on end, and did not know what to do about it or what it was for. Now I saw that the "voice" was right; it was pointless and meaningless, and more: I could make it go away by simply recognizing its uselessness, by simply seeing it as self-indulgent.

It was quite a revelation and for a second, I think, I was annoyed, at some level rather enjoying my angst, feeling perhaps that it was noble and wise and a sign of my worthiness. It would have been a different matter if I'd just been told I had cancer or my mother had just died or my child or husband were in some great trouble, but since none of this was the case, I shook my head in dismay at my foolishness—I really was chagrined that I could be such a fool—took a deep breath, and walked on, now with my mind clearing. I could not have asked for more in the way of solace if I'd taken my misery to a priest or even a psychiatrist.

I'd read Evelyn Underhill's *Mysticism* thoroughly, even made notes on it, and copied out the parts about "auditions:" "True auditions are usually heard when the mind is in a state of deep absorption without conscious thought: ... at the most favourable of all moments for contact with the transcendental world. They translate into articulate language some aspect of that ineffable apprehension of Reality which the contemplative enjoys ..." She goes on to quote St. Teresa on the subject: " ... very distinctly formed: but by the bodily ear they are not heard..." and so on. I wasn't a contemplative by any means, and I wasn't fool enough or deluded enough to think that the one Christian God with whom I'd been raised (but in whom I no longer believed) spoke to me directly, but as the "voiceless voice" was both genderless and impersonal—that is, I'd certainly never thought it was a dead relative or friend—I couldn't even begin to identify it. I didn't know from where it had come. I knew only that if I needed the voice, it seemed I could find it in the field.

Even in anger I went there. Once, filled with rage that I felt was fully justified, I was stomping through the field saying nasty things mentally about the person who'd so enraged me. I thought, This is too much, I can't endure any more, people haven't the right to treat me so badly, etc., etc., etc., and I was imploring the gods for justice, when suddenly I tripped over nothing and fell headlong into a big bed of sage. This added indignity only made me more furious, but the sage buoyed me up and I floated on it as if it were a feather bed. After a second I turned over to lie on my back, and there I rested, catching my breath, the anger slowly draining away until there was none left, and I lay there, relaxed and peaceable.

But off to my right as I fell, I'd caught a glimpse of a cluster of Amerindian women, looking like the Amerindian women of my childhood in their long dark cotton dresses, standing tight together chortling at me. They were just there, I barely saw them, and then I was in the sage and they weren't there any more. In Plains cultures, or at least among the Cree, I read later, to show anger is to make yourself ridiculous, and the appropriate response is laughter.

As well, I read that in these cultures one does not go to a sacred place to implore Spirit for assistance without first purifying oneself and that, in Plains cultures, sage may act as an agent of purification. This was surely one of the most startling and delightful of the series of rather bizarre things that happened to me in the field. By the time it happened, years into this series of events, or non-events, that I might catch a glimpse of a group of Amerindian women in the field didn't seem beyond the pale.

Knowing of the importance of the summer solstice to people all around the world, I thought perhaps if I went to certain spots in the field on that day, I might find some answers to my growing list of questions and speculations about the field. On every subsequent summer solstice when it wasn't raining or clouded over, I went there, alone or with Peter or once or twice with a friend, in hopes of discovering something striking, some lining up of significant points, perhaps revealing a petroglyph that I couldn't otherwise see, or having some animal come and talk to me as Amerindian people said they did. Maybe I would have *the* vision that would explain every-thing to me.

It was during these trips out to the field that I first noticed that the site of the stone circle on top of the flattened hill, the one I'd thought might be a burial tent for a Siksika leader, was the first place lit by the rising sun every morning, while all around it the hills and draws remained in shadows. But not once on these numerous trips out to the field did Peter and I, stationing ourselves each at what we thought to be significant points, ever discover anything new. Nothing "lined up" with anything else, the first or the last rays of light did not reveal anything in particular that we could see, nor did they receive precise rays of sunlight at sunrise or sunset as has been demonstrated at other sites. Nor did revelations of any kind strike either of us.

One summer solstice I'd slept in and missed the sunrise, and had pretty well decided not to bother for this year since it was all so hopeless anyway. The evening, though, was so still and lovely that I got on my bike and went riding on a road that passed the field. Peter was working nearby on a tractor, and as I passed the field and noticed how close it was in time to the actual moment when the sun would drop below the western horizon, on a sudden impulse I dropped my bike on the roadside, rushed across a flat area dodging greasewood and cactus, and crawled through the fence into the field. Then I hesitated, trying to decide at what point to watch the sun disappear. I walked towards the east and the long slope that led to the flattened hill where the large circle and the stone cairns at each of the four directions on the perimeter of the circle were, the hill I'd begun to think of as "the Blackfoot hill." (Although by then I knew it might be Cree or Gros Ventre or people much, much older than any of them.)

The sun was behind me, hovering just above the line of hills. Not a cloud, not the shred of a cloud, marred the clarity and luminescence of the sky in any direction. I started up the slope, and in the long gold-red rays of the sun behind me, I saw for the first time that, in fact, there was a path leading up the hill marked out by once carefully placed stones on each side of it. I had never noticed this before, but this powerful, low light made it clear for anyone to see.

I felt my heart swelling and growing light in my chest. This was something wonderful, something new. I was afraid, but I walked slowly, virtually holding my breath as if expecting at any second that an apparition might appear or that I might be struck dead on the spot for violating another sacred site. But at the top the path ended and I was still alive. On the level surface now I took a few steps forward, planning to go into the central circle which I thought might once have held a burial tent. But suddenly, looking down and ahead of my feet, I got lost. In this strong, utterly pristine, yet almost liquid, deep-red light, the circle had disappeared, or changed—I could not find it.

At my feet in front of me was a north-south ridge of embedded stone. At first I mistook it for the west perimeter of the circle, but then I saw that the line went straight north and south to the edges of the flat ridge, never curving. It was not part of any circle. I hadn't noticed this line of stone before, despite many trips to this archeological feature, and I was surprised at myself that I'd missed it despite the careful looking I'd done over the years. (I'd seen them, but in ordinary daylight they looked like the natural scatter of stones that characterized the field.) For an instant I wondered if in my haste I'd gotten lost and gone to the wrong place entirely.

I think I must have crossed the ridge and walked east a few more feet, and by doing this, managed to pick out the circle of stone I'd been looking for and relocated myself, facing west, and waiting for the sun to sink out of sight. I was afraid, but because I could see Peter a half-mile or so away on the tractor, I didn't feel I was quite alone.

But the light! The immense power of it, the way it changed the aspect of the hill completely, confusing and frightening me. I knew that the particular way the site had been changed by it on such an auspicious day was no accident, that I was far from being the first person to be caught in its rays this way. But real darkness was falling now, and I left the field as quickly as I could, rushing down the long slope, scrambling back under the fence, hurrying to my bike, and racing Peter and the tractor home.

I've puzzled often over that line of stone, which I can now make out in the grass and earth, although it still looks pretty haphazard and of no significance. But that evening on the solstice it had been the most powerful sight on that ridge, like a wall or a firm boundary. I began to wonder if it was put there deliberately to warn interlopers that they were approaching a sacred place and had better be properly humble and reverent or else should not proceed. I only know what I saw that evening, and that in ordinary light there's not a hint of any such thing.

I was beginning not merely to feel but to *know* that there was something very strange about this field. But aside from my peculiarly strong need to be in the field, and my sense of something more than rocks, grass, and animals dwelling there, I mostly left explanations aside and walked away with a huge, puzzled hollow in my head where explanations should have been. I thought that one day an explanation would occur to me, or would be handed to me, and that everything would make sense. And in the meantime, since nobody understood my experiences and was questioning, pushing, and criticizing me, making me conclude that I was simply insane or that none of it had ever happened, I left these questions hanging, and turned away, and walked on.

I no longer knew at what point the reality of the field—the snake, the coyotes, the deer, the badger, and the stone artifacts and features—might shade off into the realm that we call myth but that Amerindians know simply as creation. I, too, more often than I consciously realized, was dissolving through what I had thought was a hard line, a solid boundary, but that turned out to be amorphous, the one world as real as the other, from the Euro-American world of hard, immutable fact into the Amerindian creation that is at once physical and made of spirit.

These experiences were reward enough in themselves, but as the years passed I had this sense of being perhaps led somewhere—I couldn't begin to guess where. I hadn't forgotten my vow years earlier to try to discover the story of the field by walking it with the greatest attention and openness to whatever I might find. But if I had some glimpse of story, I also had a glimpse that this had to do with something more than only story, and I wanted to know what that was—and I wanted to know why the story mattered so much that I was being totally caught up in it.

Chapter 4

THE WILD

A FEW YEARS AGO, AFTER A LONG WEEKEND AWAY ON THE
business of literature, I was driving home, drained and weary in both
body and spirit. It was late on a November day, and it was cold, with
thin patches of snow lying on hillsides and in depressions on the
plain below them. It was foggy too, and as I approached home, on
impulse, I turned and drove past the field. When I was directly
opposite it, I stopped the car and rolled down the window to stare
at the tawny, rock-studded hills, surprised at how near they seemed
today, as if I might reach out and touch them. I sat quietly, my face
turned to them as fog and mist drifted past, breaking here and there
to reveal the slopes and then closing to obscure them again. After a
moment I heard myself breathe, "Thank you," and then turned
away to drive on.

I hadn't willed that surprising "thank you"; I didn't know why I
had said it or what it meant. The air slowly filling the truck was cold,
though, and my fingers on the steering wheel were growing numb.
In those few seconds, no explanation occurred to me, and baffled, I
rolled up the window and went on my way home.

But I did not forget the incident. I felt that *something* had happened; it must have, because spontaneously, completely without willing it, I'd found myself thanking what I had seen, as if I had been seeking respite, or comforting, or a blessing, and the hills and rocks and grass and drifting fog had given it to me. I puzzled over it, laughed a little at my tendency to seek and feel rewarded by mystery itself, and then tried to dismiss the matter. Every once in a while, though, those few moments staring out at the silent field would come back to me, and I'd puzzle over them again. But no matter how much or how long I pondered, I didn't know what it was that had happened.

One night years earlier, I had dreamt I was about to enter the field. In the dream it looked as I have described it: at the south border closest to me, a row of low hills dominated by one larger, longer, flat-topped hill sloping from east to west; behind it, a fairly level basin of wild grasses, cactus, sage, greasewood, patches of hard-pan and salt, jumbles of stones, and so on; and sloping slowly up from that, another range of higher hills and cliffs that curve around at the east and west borders to enclose the interior basin and its few small, low hills. All of it grass-covered, all of it strewn with stones of varying sizes and many colours, and having an air of wildness over and in it.

I was entering the field from the southeast corner with some trep-idation composed at least partly of fear and also of a tremulous, hesi-tant awe, as if something might happen—I did not know what. Suddenly, I saw far ahead of me in the centre of the basin, which is the centre of the field, a low, rectangular platform made of unpainted, weathered wood. I stopped, and as I watched, a manlike creature—heavy-set, powerfully built, wearing a shirt and pants with sleeves and legs torn off at the elbows and knees revealing his tremendously muscular calves and forearms, with hair longish and unkempt—strode, half-bent, out of the wild grasses, leapt onto the platform, and stalked to its centre. A voice said loudly, "*He is Lord of the Wild.*"

I woke, amazed. I thought it a wonderful concept, the revelation from somewhere deep inside me. Then I remembered that earlier I'd had a similar dream, in which I'd stopped my car at a certain spot on the dirt road that bisects the ranch, and from the nearby spring, a creature, half-man, half-beast, suddenly appeared and strode towards me through the shin-high wild grass, his ragged clothing flapping in the wind. There are few springs in a country as dry as this one, and that particular spring is famous for never having dried up once in all the years settlers were arriving in the area, not even during the "dirty thirties." Consequently, the creature's appearance there placed him in the kingdom of the gods and of supernatural beings, since from ancient times flowing water has been seen as animate and divine.

The Greeks personified the spirits of such places as nymphs. But this creature had no nymph-like qualities. As he strode towards me, I was very alarmed, and after trying frantically to get back into my car (all the doors were stuck shut) to speed away, I'd wakened.

In retrospect, in both dreams, I did not really have a sense of the creature having direct intentions to hurt me. He seemed only to be striding with great vigour and strength, a natural force, unstoppable and unequivocal, and if I was afraid, it was not precisely clear why (except that even as women love the masculine power, they also greatly and, with good reason, fear it).

I wondered and wondered about this creature, a little in awe of what my own psyche had produced, although as an avid reader of Jung I accepted this "Lord of the Wild" as an archetypal figure who had appeared from the collective unconscious. It is worth noting, though, that Jung suggests that such a figure may also represent the individual's "shadow" side, in this case, wild, powerful, determined with an innocent ruthlessness, although not malevolent, not deliberately cruel.

I wondered, too, why I hadn't dreamt of a Lady of the Wild (a creature I inadvertently picture as wearing pretty, silky, white animal skins, with a circlet of wildflowers around her brow, a sparrow twittering charmingly in her palm), but mostly I was puzzling over the prevalent notion of Nature as feminine, as Mother Earth, and wondering what it said about me that my psyche personified "wild" as masculine. "The Earth is our Mother," Amerindians say, and who should know better than they? Contemporary feminist thinkers, too, have turned back to the ancient belief of the earth as feminine and a mother. If I thought about it at all, I saw Nature as masculine. Or perhaps I meant by this only that all the Nature I knew belonged to men: as farmers or ranchers, loggers or hunters; or as adventurers in it and explorers of it. Perhaps what my dream revealed was that I saw what is *wild* in Nature as masculine: ruthless, powerful, amoral, and, in the end, untameable.

I looked in Clarissa Pinkola Estés's *Women Who Run With the Wolves: Myths and Stories of the Wild Woman Archetype*, because I remembered that she talks at length about the "wild woman" in all of us, arguing that we women need to find her in ourselves and honour her. Estés's "wild woman" is the true self that, I believe, is the life task for all of us to seek, but that is harder for women than for men because society's strictures, what one must do and be, weigh more heavily on women. As valuable as I found Estés's ideas, I knew they were in another realm of discussion and had no bearing on my "Lord of the Wild" dreams.

Then I remembered that early in our marriage, Peter had had a dream in which he was riding on the prairie and came upon a large

flat rock embedded in the grass which he'd never seen before. In it
a woman's face glittered and shone, and he rode round and round
the rock, staring at it in awe. At the time I thought his dream
reflected the new understanding dawning on a man who had
remained a bachelor in a man's world until he was forty-one and,
through his late marriage to me, was only now coming face to face
with the mysterious, but very great power of the feminine. But now,
realizing that his dream took place out on the prairie and not in the
world of the domestic more appropriate to me, I felt that perhaps it
had more to do with some concretization (possibly stirred up by our
marriage) of his primal notion of the essence of Nature. After all,
when I told Peter of my second "Lord of the Wild" dream, he
grinned, flexed his biceps teasingly, and said, "Hey, that was me!"
and for a moment I'd been half-convinced that he was the source of
my dream.

Could it be, I wondered, that the male conception of what is wild
in Nature is the feminine, and the female conception is male? And if
so, what did this mean? I thought it probably only projection. What
one truly does not understand is the essence of the other gender, and
so one projects that onto another unknown—the essence of Nature.

But this didn't satisfy me with regard to my mysterious dreams. I
wanted to understand them in terms of my fascination with Nature,
especially as it was to be found in the field, with my search for the
"root" of Nature, the true source of its wonders, rather than only in
the examination of my own psyche. No matter what Jung or anyone
else might say, I felt that there is an *out there*—a world that is not
myself—even if I wasn't at all sure of what it was constituted or of
my ability to describe it. But was it my own true self, as Jung
suggested? How could it be, I wondered, when it told me things I
didn't know? When it seemed so clearly not myself? I felt convinced,

or convinced enough, that the powerful half-man in my dreams was a signpost pointing to something "out there" that I still had to discover, just as I still had to discover what it meant that an antelope could also be a unicorn.

I went back to my books, this time abandoning psychoanalysis in favour of those thinkers pursuing concepts about Nature. Simon Schama, in *Landscape and Memory*, had discussed the archetype of the Wild Man or Wild Woman and traced its development and changes over centuries among Germans, from figures to be feared to a romanticized portrait of them as innocent and good—like my Disneyish image of the Lady of the Wild, I realized. But, in the end, Schama's remarks about the "wild man" and "wild woman" were not very helpful.

I turned then to J. E. Cirlot's *Dictionary of Symbols*, in which I read: "The image of the Wild Man or savage, covered only with a loin-cloth, or a garment of leaves or skins, is a common one in the folklore of almost every country." Which led me to the most thorough and respected source on these matters, James G. Frazer's *The Golden Bough*, originally published in 1890. He recounts at some length rituals in which the "wild man" (a young man dressed in green boughs, also sometimes called "the Green Man") is chased and mock-killed in spring ceremonies of peasant people all over northern Europe.

Cirlot offers little explanation, but Frazer traces such figures far back in history and says that originally they were human representatives of the tree spirit, a God-King on whom the fruitfulness of Nature depended. Each year he had to be ritually killed before his gifts flagged so that a fresh king with more abundant powers could be established.

No longer sure I knew myself what I meant by the word "wild," I turned to the final authority on the English language, the *Oxford*

English Dictionary, for a basic definition. It said: "Of a place or region: uncultivated or uninhabited; hence, waste, desert, desolate." Wild animals are described as "undomesticated." "Wilderness," on the other hand, it defines as "a wild or uncultivated region or tract of land, uninhabited, or inhabited only by wild animals." But it begins its definition by saying, "The problem of the ulterior relations of this word is complicated by *uncertainty as to its primary meaning*" (italics mine).

Whoever the figure in my dreams was, he was not constructed by humans to satisfy their needs as Frazer's "wild man" was, but appeared as a natural force, or as an embodiment of a natural force, that is, an embodiment of certain qualities of Nature, with no interest in benevolence towards humans—with no interest in humans at all. Ah, I thought, perhaps this is all we mean by "wild"—alien, unknowable. But then, why do we yearn for it so much?

It occurred to me to wonder what "wild" might mean to the people who, for at least ten thousand years and possibly longer, had been inhabitants of this continent and who had learned to survive here without "benefit" of European culture—without a written language, guns, horses, cities, or man-made cathedrals in which to worship. I thought that perhaps the people or peoples who had made the stone circles in the field, who had left behind the stone cylinder and sphere, did not have such a concept, at least not in connection with Nature.

Naturally, I already knew about the Sasquatch (from a Coast Salish language, the word *saskehavas*), or in the United States, Bigfoot, and his counterpart in Asia, the Abominable Snowman (a translation of Tibetan *metohkangmi*—foul snowman), also called

Yeti. The Sasquatch is a creature of the peoples of the Pacific Northwest, though as Robert Pyle, after doing extensive research, concludes in *Where Bigfoot Walks: Crossing the Great Divide*, "Few cultures lack a human-faced hairy monster, giant, or wild man."

I also read about the Kwakiutl figures (also Pacific Northwest coast) called Dzonoqua (giant) and Bukwus (ghost chief), interpreted by anthropologists as the Wild Woman and Wild Man of the forest, but with whom the Kwakiutl "consorted" and with whom an ancestor of one clan had mated. These seemed slightly different in concept to me, since I didn't think anyone human was said to have mated with a Sasquatch. And then in the northern centre of the continent, there is the Wetigo, or Wihtiko, who is a cannibal or who makes people into cannibals so that they beg to be killed before they kill others. This creature seems to be a sort of embodiment of winter—his/her mouth in some versions is all frost and ice—at a time when starvation was the great scourge of the people.

Where or how the Sasquatch made the jump into non-Amerindian folklore is not recorded. Non-Amerindian believers describe Sasquatch as seven to twelve feet tall, and a manlike, upright creature covered with fur or hair except on his face and palms—"hairy giant" is the frequent appellation—and whose footprints are as long as eighteen inches. He is believed to live in the vast, dense forests of the coastal area, and is said to run and hide at the sight of humans, and may therefore reasonably be called a "wild man." Although there are inveterate Sasquatch hunters, most of those whose belief systems are rooted in Europe think of him as not real. Even paleontologists who have been interested in him as a possible relict species of hominoid seem largely to have given up that search, in the total absence of a specimen.

And yet, the flesh-and-blood Sasquatch of the non-Amerindian believers is not at all the Sasquatch of Amerindians. The translation across cultures appears to me to be inexact, not the least because in the culture of non-Amerindian believers the Sasquatch exists as an amazing anomaly, virtually without context, while in Amerindian cultures he appears within the continuum of existence and as a part of the created world.

The more I think about the Sasquatch as non-Amerindians understand him, the more I think of him as an inevitable construct for a people arriving on a new continent about which they knew nothing, refusing to learn from its inhabitants, continuing to declare the continent as "empty" and "untouched," despite the evidence of its far-flung population whose ancient ability to survive on the land's resources should have been obvious to the new arrivals. Exhilarated as they were, the adventurers and settlers had to have been—at root—afraid: afraid of the vast distances, of the mysterious, deep and dark forests, of the wild rivers, and of the immense, markerless sea of grass that was the Great Plains. They did not know, when they set out on a journey or when they began to chop down trees to make a clearing for a farm, what they might expect to encounter; they did not know the animals, birds, or insects, or what weather might be expected from a cloud formation or a colour in the sky.

And so, afraid but determined, they went about their business. "Wild," to them, meant dangerous, unknown, possibly unimaginable, not amenable to reason, heartless, if not downright malevolent. And out of this, or versions of it, as the years passed, I speculate, they began to accept a creature conveniently already named—the Sasquatch—as an embodiment of all their fears that they could not define.

But, interesting as all this speculation was, it seemed to be taking me even farther from an interpretation of my own "Lord of the

Wild," for my dream creature wasn't covered in hair or fur; he didn't walk like an ape or look much like one except for his extreme muscularity. He was clearly primarily human, even dressed in human garments. The Amerindian Sasquatch, too, I had to dismiss as not helpful in understanding the creature of my dreams. As I kept on with my search, slowly I began to see that traditionally Amerindians do not make a separation as we do between the mythological and the physical worlds. They see them as one world. This is easy to say but very hard for those of us of a different race and culture and raised within the Christian worldview to understand. In light of my slowly dawning recognition of the Amerindian worldview, I saw that perhaps I didn't at all understand what they might mean, when and if—if the word even occurred in their own languages—they use the word "wild."

In my search through my books, I had stumbled upon a surprising quote from T. C. McLuhan's *Touch the Earth*, by an Amerindian much closer to our own time and with perhaps *too* much experience of the invaders' culture: Luther Standing Bear (1868–1939), a Brulé Lakota who, although raised traditionally, lived a large part of his adult life in the general world:

> Only to the white man was nature a "wilderness" and only to him was the land "infested" with "wild" animals and "savage" people. To us it was tame. Earth was bountiful and we were surrounded with the blessings of the Great Mystery. Not until the hairy man from the East came and with brutal frenzy heaped injustices upon us and the families that we loved was it "wild" for us. When the very animals of the forest began fleeing from his approach, then it was that for us the "Wild West" began.

At first I didn't know how to reconcile this profoundly bitter statement with the thrill and mystery of Dzonoqua and Bukwus and Sasquatch, and a people who, in their histories, told of mating with such creatures. It is true that Chief Luther Standing Bear was not from the Kwakiutl and Coast Salish peoples, and from a very different way of life on the open, unforested Great Plains, but the absolute familiarity of Amerindians with their own terrain, flora and fauna, and their belief in all aspects of Nature as ensouled, appears to remain roughly the same throughout Amerindian cultures. I suspected this was a case where an Amerindian, understanding the European worldview, was trying to speak—for the sake of better understanding—in the terms non-Amerindian people would use. Surely, I thought, this is not how he would have put this to his own people in his own language. ("Likely but unprovable" was how an eminent archeologist responded to my thesis.)

Although the sentiment in Standing Bear's remark made a kind of good sense to me, I didn't entirely trust it as an accurate expression of what it was Amerindians felt they had lost or had seen spoiled by the coming of Europeans to their world. I am also conscious here of the fact that I am making a discrimination which very likely only an Amerindian has the right to make—that is, that I am a non-Amerindian announcing to the world what is an authentic Amerindian view and what is not. This being unacceptable, I offer it only as a suggestion and stand to be corrected. The remark also contains so many ideas that in order to understand its implications thoroughly, it would have to be deconstructed phrase by phrase. Possibly what we are facing here is an unbridgeable gap between two cultures and two worldviews.

George E. Tinker, an Osage, writing an entry on religion in the *Encyclopedia of North American Indians*, points to two worldviews:

"All of the created world is ... seen as alive, sentient, and filled with spiritual power ...." In contrast, we make a sharp distinction as to what is ensouled, for the most part attributing souls only to human beings. That is, we don't attribute "spiritual power" to any visible part of creation but human beings. And if, for Amerindians, everything is filled with spiritual power or ensouled, then surely in such a worldview nothing can be "wild," at least not as we use the word?

Now I had spent a good many years living in the country and a part of every day walking on uninhabited and unploughed terrain, which had opened me to a whole new understanding of what constitutes Nature and raised the question of what we mean in our culture when we speak of "the wild." Increasingly, as the foregoing discussion shows, it had begun to seem to me that our ideas about this concept were murky, and with the advent of the environmental movement, in the beginning consisting chiefly of men—its most important figures are still mostly men—they became even murkier. Not surprisingly, there were conflicts between Amerindians and Inuit and environmentalists. If the two groups understood the natural world in the same way, there would be no conflicts; where there were, environmentalists clearly belonged in the camp of all North Americans of European, Christian background. Outrage seemed to be their defining characteristic, and this I attributed to the fact that their leaders and creators were disaffected men.

I had written with cynicism about men who think "wild" can be found only in hard-to-reach, little-known places like the mountain ranges of Tibet, the snow and ice of the high Arctic, the jungles of Borneo, or the great deserts of Asia and Africa. They arrive as adventurers of one sort or another—having a sense of superiority to the local people who, in fact, live there *all their lives* without expensive equipment or having supplies airlifted in, a mind-boggling vanity on the part of the adventurers. Such attitudes smacked to me of nothing so much as mere elitism, of masculine arrogance at its worst. In particular, it meant that farmers, ranchers, fishermen were presumed to be excluded from knowing anything about Nature, despite having lived in it all their lives. I should here add that I do not by any means put all the diverse people called "environmentalists" in this camp.

After all, I had not needed an education in science, a lot of money or even any money at all, or expensive special equipment to walk now and then in my field, where I felt myself to be in another realm from that of everyday life, and about which, out of extensive experience and in all sincerity, I use the word "wild." And to suggest that Peter, in his more than sixty years of sojourning on the unploughed prairie, had not experienced "the wild" struck me as ridiculous.

And yet, if I declare a particular field to be "wild" which motorized vehicles on homely errands drive within sight and sound of every day, I cannot mean the same thing as those men who, in their search for something "wild" enough, seek out vast tracts of uninhabited land—or what they think of as uninhabited—that is, undisturbed by humans or, at least, by Europeans. This is by definition land that is very difficult to traverse and remote from large populations. (If it weren't, it would be inhabited by non-indigenous people, and there would be cities on it or nearby.) I began to suspect that for many, "the wild" has been translated into proving one's manhood through overcoming physical difficulties in places where there's no help to be had if things go wrong.

To such people my field would not qualify as "wild" because at a mere hundred-and-some acres it's too small, too close to civilization, and even though much less disturbed than the surrounding fields, has nonetheless been disturbed by the first settlers, who have crossed it (there is a fading wagon track through the field and, at one fence, a depression where one of them once had a dug-out barn) and in the past used it for grazing land for their semi-domesticated animals.

Thoreau said, "In wildness is the preservation of the world," not "wilderness," specifying that he means a quality to be found certainly within wilderness, but not necessarily only there. What this quality is he does not specifically say, assuming, as we all seem to, that we know what is meant by the word. But at least one writer, Roger DiSilvestro, in his book *Reclaiming the Last Wild Places: A New Agenda for Biodiversity*, equates it with biodiversity: "Protection of biodiversity, of wildness ...."

In the end, the essence of the meaning of the word "wild" is an unknowable, at least partly because the moment it is known, it is no longer wild. Still, we search out what we think of as wild, and we go there, regardless of what our presence might do to it, and it takes quite a while and quite a few visitors before we cease to call it "wild." We must therefore, when we describe a place or an animal as wild, mean something more than merely undomesticated, or uninhabited by humans, but having also some undescribed, possibly indescribable, essence that is present, of another dimension perhaps, something that cannot be known without destroying it, or that cannot be known at all. In the nineteenth century, Thoreau had written: "It is in vain to dream of a wildness distant from ourselves. It is the bog in our brain and bowels, the primitive vigor of Nature in us, that inspires that dream." For once, I'm not sure Thoreau was right.

I stumbled across this story: in 1994 a group of a dozen conservationists, scientists, two artists, and a photographer set out to explore the Kitlope ("people of the rocks"), the traditional land of the Haisla people of Kitimaat Village in northwestern British Columbia. The Kitlope is 100,000 hectares of remote coastal temperate rainforest, mountainous, and a watershed, referred to by the author of an article about the trip which he accompanied as "the drop side of yonder."

The expedition members were extensively and expensively equipped with the best gear for wilderness adventure, and as people in love with wilderness, experienced with it, and also well-equipped with scientific knowledge about aspects of Nature, from professional river-runners and a river geomorphologist to botanist and archeologist, they expected to explore the area and to have a bracing and enlightening time.

In fact, the Kitlope easily defeated them, expensive equipment, experience with wilderness, scientific knowledge, and all. In fear for their very lives if they continued to try to go upstream on the Kitlope River, they had to stop where they were and call for helicopter pickup.

I asked a Haisla woman, one of a group of Amerindian people who succeeded in saving the Kitlope from the logging industry, what she thought about this trip. Why had these well-equipped and experienced adventurers failed? Something that looked to me like a mixture of contempt and anger quickly crossed her face as she turned her head away from me, smoothed out her expression and turned back, saying tightly, "They went in the wrong season. That's all I'll say."

After all, her people—in a clear case of indigenous capability triumphing over technology and its apparently inseparable hubris—had been at home for nine thousand years in the Kitlope without life jackets, rubber rafts, and flown-in, freeze-dried food. Her anger at the adventurers' arrogance might have been a part of what she held back in answering my question, but I am more inclined to believe that she was thinking of her people's traditional knowledge, including—or perhaps even especially—spiritual knowledge, about the world of the Kitlope.

Even the author of the article about the trip, writing well after the experience, says:

> To avoid "big trouble" here, I suspect, demands a type and measure of respect we have yet to show.... When they [the Henaaksiala, a branch of the Haisla] came to the upper river, it would have been for a specific reason, in the right season, in the right way, with the right attitude.

Doubtless this was what their Haisla informants told the adventurers after they'd emerged, bedraggled, chastened, and considering themselves profoundly fortunate to have got out with nothing worse than damaged or lost equipment and a couple of sprained ankles. The Kitlope represented to them "wild" of the deepest kind—it ought to have been (although I doubt it was) even satisfying to have been defeated by it. While to the Haisla, it was something else entirely.

Recently I dreamt I was with a group of people out on the prairie. We looked up and saw low in the sky a pair of giant, tawny-coloured paws of some member of the cat family, probably a lion. The paws were placed side by side and motionless, the claws retracted out of sight. The rest of the animal was hidden by drifting cloud, but as we looked, the mist drifted apart in patches and we saw the animal's face and some of its chest, although not its mane, which remained obscured by clouds. It was seated on its haunches, its eyes closed in repose, although it was not asleep, its mouth closed and still, its expression solemn. Its fur was the normal, tawny lion colour, but I noticed especially the odd lack of vibrancy to its colour.

When I woke, although I remembered the dream clearly and in detail, it did not strike me as being of any import and I paid little attention to it. It was not until a day or two had passed that I began to wonder what such a dream could mean—portents in the sky, mirabilia, and so on. I started to search my books for clues as to its meaning, and then, failing to find anything very significant, mentioned it in passing to my older sister. She suggested at once the sphinx, and that seemed very apt to me because of the association with stillness and mystery, and then the zodiacal sign of Leo, which aroused no echoes in me.

I began to search my own psyche for associations. I had found in one of my books that in some systems the lion symbolized earthly power or even, simply, earth. I thought that the closed eyes, the stillness of a creature who was clearly alive, symbolized mystery, the silence of the Great Mystery, the silence of the gods.

Then I remembered my strange experience that day a year or two before, of coming home depleted both spiritually and physically, passing the field, and rolling down my window to the snow-spotted, tawny hills and the drifting cloud and mist, and then finding myself thanking someone or something. The memory jolted me: that dull tawny colour, the silence, the stillness. I could feel the way in which the two experiences matched, even the curiously dead tone of the lion's fur, I realized, was exactly the colour of the sun-cured grasses of the hills from late summer until the snow fell. But I couldn't quite put my finger on the connection.

In the real-life experience, I had not been able to understand what it was that had happened, although by then I knew that field was something extraordinary. In fact, by the time I had the Lord of the Wild dreams, although the field was also my Nature school, my place where I enjoyed the outdoors in the ordinary sense, and where I took exercise, it *had* become my place of sanctuary, of solace, and of prayer. It had become my church, and I went there in silence, with reverence, and in awe, hoping to make a connection with—*something*—if not the gods, then at least with spirit or with a spirit, although of what or whom I didn't know, but had thought must be the spirit or essence of Nature. In the midst of the questioning I've spoken of, walking in the field had gone from being an enjoyable way to pass the time—even if sometimes I had to use all my resolve in conquering my tiredness sufficiently to get there—to an activity that called on all my resources of concentration, energy, and devotion.

What I found in the field, I began to see, was *presence*, but it was presence beyond that of the animals who made it home; it was *presence* that I was nowhere near ready to name precisely or even describe. It had taken me months—during which I mostly didn't think of the dream at all though my subconscious life was busy internalizing all these chaotic thoughts and meagre pieces of research—before I suddenly understood: The lion in the sky represented this farther, unseen *presence* that I was beginning to accept was in the field.

A unicorn, a Lord of the Wild, a sphinx: I was beginning to think that each of them in its own way represented this quality of *consciousness* I was finding, but which I couldn't define or name, that we call "the wild."

Stone

Chapter 5

OLD MAN ON HIS BACK

AS LONG AS ANYONE COULD REMEMBER SINCE THE COMING of the first European settlers, a certain large hill on the point of a great lifting of the land west of the Butala ranch has been called "Old Man On His Back." Wallace Stegner, the American writer who lived in this area from 1914 to 1920, mentions passing Old Man On His Back in those years on the way to the family homestead along the Montana border on the Saskatchewan side. I recall it as being one of the first landmarks pointed out to me when I came here, and I remembered it not only because the feature itself is so striking but also because its name is so unusual.

When I asked where the name had come from, I was told that, viewed from the right position, the outline of the hill formed the silhouette of an old man lying on his back. Over the years, I'd looked at the hill from all available directions and had never seen that silhouette. Peter admitted he'd never been able to either, although I'd heard others claim they had. Privately I concluded that either my eyesight was wanting or they were kidding themselves.

In 1996, Peter and I signed an agreement in which we donated some of our best native grassland to the Nature Conservancy of

Canada. The conservancy then purchased the rest of the deeded land (not including the parcel of land where the field is) and, in the same comprehensive agreement, became legal lessor of the ten thousand acres of Crown land (through the government department Saskatchewan Environment and Resource Management, or SERM) on which the Butalas had for many years run cattle and horses. It was a complicated agreement, which, as Peter likes to say, "took two years and five lawyers" to work out.

In essence, we had sold the ranch to the Nature Conservancy of Canada and had then leased it back for five years to give us time to wind down our ranching operation and the Nature Conservancy time to consolidate its position as the new owners and managers, in conjunction with SERM. The place that had always been "the ranch" to me and "home" or "Divide" to Peter (after the hamlet four miles from their house where Peter had gone to school, so named because it is on the continental divide) had officially become the Old Man On His Back Prairie and Heritage Preserve.

For thirty years, as Peter grew older, he had mulled over the possible ways in which he could "save the grass," his quandary being that most of his assets were in the land he owned. Since otherwise he hadn't enough money on which to retire, he had to find a way to raise his "retirement fund" without selling this large preserve of original native prairie, for which he had a deep, genuine, and abiding love, to someone who would destroy it.

As I've said, from its settlement until the fifties, southwest Saskatchwan had been largely ranchland. It was only with the advent of huge farming equipment and the expanding world market for grains that people saw an opportunity to move out of the almost exclusively hand-to-mouth existence that had been the case since the arrival of the settlers at the turn of the century. They began to plough up their land, at first a field here and a field there, and then more, and then still more, until places which had been ranches became the headquarters of mixed-farming operations—the growing of grains and raising of livestock together. Finally, some of the largest holdings became exclusively farms, with every last inch of land ploughed and seeded to cereal and "pulse" crops—legumes such as peas, beans, and lentils. (The name is from the Latin *puls*, a porridge of meal and legumes which is mentioned in the Bible.)

The last Saskatchewan stronghold of the original northern Great Plains grass—called "shortgrass" by the local people and "mixed grass" by the scientists—was vanishing. And vanishing to such a degree that it has been said that few places on earth have been changed so much by human hands as southern Saskatchewan. Land in native grass, in the seventies and eighties, was considered to be about 20 per cent of what it had been before the arrival of the settlers and, since it decreases every year, must now be considerably less than that.

The potential buyers for the Butala ranch were Hutterite colonies, who are large-scale farmers, or other big farmers, whether incorporated or not, or local agricultural people who would subdivide it, some using it as grazing land and some ploughing and farming it. Whoever the purchasers might be, if they were ranchers, they almost certainly would have overgrazed it because land taxes and grazing rental fees are too high for the low productivity of land in the light brown soils zone with an annual precipitation of about twelve inches. (Peter feels it takes forty to fifty acres to keep one cow, although most people nonetheless have a much higher stocking-rate.) And seriously overgrazed grassland might as well be ploughed and seeded, because for it to return to its former, healthy state would take more than a human lifetime. We can't be sure if it would ever return to the same composition and proportions of grasses as it originally had.

Knowing all of this, and approaching retirement age, Peter cast about for a way to save his grass without us spending our old age in penury. It was then we approached the Nature Conservancy of Canada, who approached the Saskatchewan government to see if such a project would be feasible. The rest, you might say, is history.

There was, however, another matter Peter and I had not counted on and which took me, if not Peter, completely by surprise. It was the degree and intensity of the resistance of some local people to the project. The Nature Conservancy had set up an advisory committee whose purpose was to counsel the new owners as to the best way to run the project to achieve the goals of saving this stand of native prairie and all the animals, insects, and birds who made their homes in it, while at the same time finding a way *through agricultural use* to make it financially self-supporting—two goals which in this area are nearly always mutually incompatible. If they were compatible, there would be a good deal more native grass around. Peter had succeeded only because he had forgone a potentially larger income in order to save the grass and because he had married late and had no children.

Representatives of all the agencies who had funded the project sat on the board, as well as the Nature Conservancy, Peter and me, people from the local governments and tourism agencies, and other organizations which traditionally had a role in determining the provincial government's policies towards the use of its grassland. Since part of the purpose of this board was to keep local people fully informed and to give them the opportunity to express their views about the project, we were taken by surprise when the inevitable and expected local grumblings escalated suddenly to a well-organized public protest meeting.

By this time, however, the contract had been legally completed, and since no such arrangement involving Crown land had been done before in the province, all parties involved had bent over backwards to fulfil every legal requirement, that is, not only to have behaved with complete legality but to have been seen to have done so—so that no matter how much protest there might be, the preserve itself was never in jeopardy.

Some of the arguments against the preserve—for example, that all that land would now sit idle when people were crying for land to plough or graze—were simply wrong. But the largest degree of antagonism seemed to be provoked by the involvement of the provincial Crown corporation, Sask Power, which, we were amazed to discover, in some areas was hated.

The reasons for this weren't clear to me. All I could think of was how grateful rural people had been when our former provincial premier and national hero Tommy Douglas, whose greatest contribution to this country was Medicare, had eventually brought electricity to all the farms in the province with the Rural Electrification Act of 1949. I remember hearing him talk about how proud he was to do that, largely because, he said, it reduced the hard labour of farm women. I began slowly to understand that the anger in this regard had to do with people seeing this as the spending of their fees paid for power on something they didn't want, and failing to understand that all corporate despoilers of the environment are required by the federal government to support environmental projects to help make up for the damage they do elsewhere.

It was around this time that I began to comprehend the single most vital fact about rural life: in the end, *everything is about land*. To understand any rural community (of non-Amerindian people, that is), it is necessary to understand the dynamics of land ownership. The families with the most social status are those who have been on land in the district longest and/or those who own the most land, large land ownership, of course, usually signifying wealth. This means that those who do not own land—teachers, clergymen, working people—can never have the status in the community of those who do (and quite conceivably, especially if they're urban-raised, never quite understand why), and no greater disaster can befall a man than to lose his land either through the commonplace rural family squabbles or through an unpayable debt load.

It means, too, that landowners are vehement about their right to do with their land whatever they choose: to plough land so marginal it can't grow a crop or to overgraze destructively. No one can simply forbid the owner to do so. Governments, alarmed by the effects of soil erosion, pollution through the application of chemical fertilizers and sprays, compaction and the loss of fertility, have to devise indirect methods of affecting land use, such as changing crop insurance or land taxation rules. The individual landowner, subject to payment of land taxes (and the Noxious Weeds Act designed by farmers to force other farmers into controlling certain weeds on their property), is king on his own land.

When farming equipment was smaller and less technological, less damage was done to the land, both because there weren't enough seasonal days for a farmer with small equipment (or horses) to plough and seed a large area of land, and because the machinery itself, being relatively lightweight and less efficient, did not damage the ground as much. Nor were there farm chemicals to pollute the environment until after the Second World War. Pollution and the loss of biodiversity through the ploughing of the grasslands affect everyone, whether city-based or not. The fact is that when rural men pursue the goals of self-aggrandizement through land ownership and wealth, they radically affect the entire country's non-renewable resources.

And yet the people of southwest Saskatchewan as a group are not wealthy. Farm size continues to grow unchecked, small farms are disappearing, rural depopulation is accelerating, and the average age of the Saskatchewan farmer is fifty-eight years. Almost everyone views the future in this rural area with considerable trepidation, as they either scramble to become bigger or see themselves disappearing within the next few years. (As I write this, the price of a bushel of wheat is lower than it was in the 1920s.) In view of this major disaster, actually merely another in a long string of periodic disasters since the arrival of the settlers around 1900, many are facing bankruptcy, and many more live in fear for what the next season will bring.

In such a climate, a well-known environmental agency suddenly arriving in their midst, just one more agency whose purpose appears to be the destruction of the livelihood of all people making a living directly off the land, must surely have sparked great fear, which expressed itself in a series of complaints and arguments against the establishment of the Old Man On His Back Prairie and Heritage Preserve. There were reasons to object, ranging from the effects of that ubiquitous little green monster—after all, Peter had found a way to have his cake and eat it too—to the astonishing distrust of Sask Power. But, in my opinion, the greatest concern of those who objected was that this project brought the much-feared environmental movement right into the heart of the community. Yet I don't recall this subject coming up once in conversations where neighbours tried to explain their objections.

Since there are so few controls on the landowner beyond the community's disapproval (which works for many people but has absolutely no effect on the worst offenders) and the requirements of the market, any environmental organization whose primary aim is preserving biodiversity is bound to be viewed with, at the least, apprehension and, at most, with hatred. (Peter was told second- or third-hand that someone in a nearby community was threatening to kill him for doing this.) It seems to me that a significant portion of the opposition was based on the fear of this nebulous bogeyman, the environmentalist, seen as just one more alien force poised to hasten the demise of the community. Yet no one spoke publicly about it, because everyone knew that wider public opinion was not on their side and because they were afraid of what even saying the words out loud might unleash on them.

In considering the environmentalists' reputations as over-educated, urban do-gooders, whose ignorance about the contingencies of rural life—of even the way of life—is monumental, we could not blame our neighbours for that fear. Ranchers and farmers have watched with horror as loggers were driven from the forest, trappers from their traplines, and fishermen from the sea, their once honourable hard labour denigrated, their lives shattered by unemployment and its accompanying effects of poverty, shame, and family disintegration. (Their own complicity in this is another story, or perhaps another part of this story which hasn't been written yet.)

Maybe even that would have been bearable if those responsible for the disenfranchising were themselves engaged as loggers, fishermen, or trappers and understood such peoples' body of specialized knowledge; or if alternatives to making a living not entirely laughable had been offered; or if recognition had been given to the value of their labour, to its historicity, its necessity in the development of this nation—recognition of the fact that the country's wealth came originally from its primary resources. Or if those thus disenfranchised had been given genuinely viable alternatives.

It occurs to me, though, that surely if agricultural people felt absolutely certain in their hearts that they weren't hurting the environment or destroying all prairie biodiversity, they wouldn't have minded a preserve in their midst. But, as with loggers, fishermen, and trappers, they saw a group of people much better off economically than themselves and too frequently speaking scientific-sounding jargon, poised, as they thought, to destroy them.

On the other hand, there is overgrazed grassland all over the West, where every last centimetre, including land the farmer doesn't own, such as road allowances and ditches, has been ploughed and seeded to cash crops, removing habitat for animals, birds, insects, and plants. And only organic farmers don't use chemical fertilizers and various pesticides and herbicides that pollute the air, soil, surface water, and probably even the water table, not to mention killing off everything else from insects to birds and small animals.

Greed, since we're dealing with the human species, certainly plays a part in some of these decisions, but more often such practices are followed because feeding your children still seems like a good idea, because farm and ranch families have always-increasing land taxes and lease fees to pay, machinery to pay for, cattle and land loans to make payments on. To make the shift from conventional farming to organic farming takes capital, a punitive amount of belt-tightening, and, especially, years, while the land becomes slowly pollutant-free. It also takes study, and that takes a certain amount of courage and a lot of support from family, friends, and neighbours, which, according to what I hear, is usually not forthcoming. The practice of conventional agriculture is a force almost impossible to resist both for practical and historical reasons.

Few ranchers, who must have most of their land in grass, would overgraze it if land taxes and lease fees were not so high. In the western United States, where hatred of the ranching community is widespread for reasons having to do with the Bureau of Land Management and with water rights, a history not applicable in Canada, environmental agencies have urged governments to raise grazing fees in order to drive ranchers out of business. The effect instead, as any rancher might have told them, has been for ranchers to fill their fields with even more cattle to provide the necessary income to pay the increased fees and taxes, resulting, of course, in even worse overgrazing.

And as Peter likes to point out, the cash value of land today is to a large degree determined by economic forces having nothing to do with it rather than by the productive worth of the land. It has to do with its distance from markets and with a municipality's need to raise tax money, with factors such as the need of the wealthy to find tax havens and to make investments. Five to ten acres with a dwelling on it in the Muskoka region of Ontario, not used for agricultural productivity, is worth around $250,000, while our agriculturally viable thirteen-thousand-acre cattle ranch was worth only slightly more than double that. And land used for acreages outside Calgary is highly valued for its proximity to the city, not for its potential agricultural productivity. Land is viewed by the dominant culture as a commodity like any other commodity.

In addition, agricultural people, in a much more direct fashion than any other group of working people from lawyers to biologists, are facing globalization and its effects. Market forces are erasing at a stupefying rate all the cogs that kept the small family farmer or rancher operating. Railway branchlines and small local elevators are being closed down, and government subsidies such as the historic Crow Rate are gone. In local communities, support systems such as farm suppliers and dealers are consolidating in bigger centres, and rural people are being driven out of the countryside in record numbers.

The result is a rapidly accelerating increase in farm size, and with increases in farm size comes the use of bigger and bigger equipment. In the early days, a farmer using a four- or eight-horse hitch and a gang plough in a day could plough something like two and a half to four acres—the old farmers used to figure, I'm told, "eight rounds before dinner and eight rounds after"—while with today's large equipment, in one day a farmer can plough or summerfallow four hundred acres. By himself he can handle much more land, and the cost of such equipment—a quarter of a million dollars or more— virtually requires that he have much more. But such huge equipment has no regard for, or knowledge of, the ground, the earth, and its ecology that a small farmer had. In fact, farming technology has now reached the day of robot equipment, where the farmer won't even be in the field as he ploughs it.

When we lose small farms with their small equipment, we are losing more than merely population: We are losing a base of knowledge about Nature at a local level that cannot be replicated in any other way, scientists and environmentalists notwithstanding. With the loss of small local elevators and their replacement by distant enormous inland terminals, with the increase in farm size, and with globalization of the economy, nobody has any interest any more in the production of a traditional small farm. Only large amounts count. The day of the family farm is over, the mourning is already taking place.

Historically, life here in southwest Saskatchewan, some of the driest and most drought-prone land in the too-dry and drought-prone

Palliser Triangle (defined by Palliser as a triangle with its base the American-Canadian border between 100 and 114 degrees longitude and its apex at 52 degrees latitude), hasn't been easy since the advent of the first settlers. To understand this, it is necessary to recognize that the Canadian West was never opened so that poor Europeans might have a better life through having land of their own, although poor Europeans might have been led to believe this. It was opened for purely political and financial reasons: to keep the Americans from taking over this so-called empty area and to provide markets for eastern interests. In Western Canada, settlers came from Europe *from the very beginning* as people who would be expected to grow crops primarily for sale. That is, the family farm was always seen by governments, and eventually by farmers, as a business. Naturally, this imperative had a profound effect on how land itself was and is viewed by farmers and ranchers—as a commodity, and the more of it the better.

With such a beginning it's hardly surprising that the land is not, for the most part, cherished by those of us whose cultural roots are in Europe in the way it should be—for its own sake, for the value inherent in its natural state—and that land in its original state, native grass of good quality, is disappearing at an alarming pace. And yet agricultural people feel themselves trapped in a situation from which they see no way out, no matter how much they may dislike and worry about how they treat the land.

The history of non-indigenous relationship with land is not a happy one. From the time of the arrival of the settlers, the land itself has suffered, biodiversity has suffered, beauty has suffered, peace and solitude and the necessary quest for "the wild" as it is found in Nature have suffered. Native people say that the land is sacred, but if it is sacred to non-natives, despite all those agricultural people who love life on the land such as it is for them, and who deplore what they feel they *must* to do it, it is sacred, for the most part, only with regard to the rights of private ownership and its capacity to be converted to cash.

In all of this I refer to men, for it seems that all land belongs to men. By this I mean not only the custom of primogeniture or some variation of it (the usual way of passing land from one generation to the next, that is, from man to man), but the fact that when women are widowed or where there is no son to inherit the land, almost none of the women actually take control of it. They are expected to marry as soon as is decent—many are said to receive some very surprising proposals—to rent it out to other men, to find a male relative who will farm it for them, or to hire a man who can run it for them until, where there is one, their eldest son is of age to take over.

Where women not only own but attempt to take control of their farms and ranches, I'm told, they can expect a certain amount of harassment from those men who feel themselves entitled to the land. At a farm women's conference some years ago, a widow spoke about her experiences in trying to run their farm after her husband died. She spoke of not knowing how to build a barbed-wire fence and described how her father, who had cancer, sat in the half-ton directing her and her young son as they worked at it. Every day a neighbour drove by and watched from a distance. The day the fence was finished, he phoned the woman to tell her that she'd have to move that fence, since it was on his land, a charge which, of course, turned out to be untrue and constituted mere vicious harassment.

If so few women have control of agricultural land, it is pointless to try to talk about whether farm-and-ranch women approach land differently than their men do. They talk about it differently than men do, but then they are not the ones who spend their days out on it; nor do they have the most responsibility for making it produce or for making decisions about it. Perhaps, if they did have equal control of land *as the source of their livelihood,* they would behave exactly as most non-aboriginal men do towards it, although possibly they'd feel less competitive about it.

Nonetheless, there are farmers and ranchers who do genuinely love their land, and love best about agricultural life the clean air, the clear view of the rising of the sun and the moon, the return of the ducks and geese, the deer grazing under the window in the early morning, the coyote loping across the field, or the antelope racing up a hillside, who love even the little skunk that lives under the barn and feeds with the barn cats every morning. Who love also the smell of the earth in the spring, the blessed solitude, the sense of life on the land as the right way, the way people were meant to live—as a part of Nature, fitting themselves to her cycles and to her demands, and thus understanding even time differently than the urban born and bred. This is true, and it is good and beautiful, but it is also rarer and rarer. When this generation of rural people dies off, perhaps it will be gone for good, and so we fervently hope and pray our small preserve will help to save those old memories and attitudes.

It was not until we began talks with the Nature Conservancy that I realized that Old Man On His Back was not merely a nearby landmark, but that the Butala ranch was actually situated on the Old Man On His Back plateau. Since the hill itself was about ten miles from the ranch, on a road we didn't often take, we rarely passed the hill. But Peter and I were delighted when the conservancy decided to use the name for its new preserve despite, or more likely because of, its oddness. Odder still was the fact that almost no one could make out the feature by which it was thought to have obtained its name.

Once the preserve was a fact, all the agencies involved began to make plans for a big inauguration ceremony and celebration to be held first on the land itself and then in a nearby local hall. Peter and I had waited a long time for this moment, and we could hardly contain our excitement. We were asked how we would feel about inviting the people of Nekaneet, the only reserve in all of southwest Saskatchewan other than a very small Lakota reserve east at Wood Mountain, to take part in our celebration. Since the late 1880s, Nekaneet and his followers had stubbornly, at great cost to themselves, stayed in the Cypress Hills even though they had no reserve until 1913, when they were finally given a tiny one, which some years later was expanded a bit. They were the only Amerindian people who refused to be driven out after the signing of Treaty Four in 1874, and so had been here since long before the arrival of the first settlers. (In September of 1992 they settled their land claims and began to buy land.)

We thought their presence to help us celebrate the establishment of the preserve would be absolutely fitting and right, and when word came back that they would come and would hold a sweat, a feast, and a round dance, it seemed to us that everything Peter had for so long dreamt of was falling into place as it should.

A few days before the big event was to take place, an elder came to meet with us so that he might pick the best location for these festivities. On the drive down from the reserve, someone asked the elder if he knew anything about this strange name: Old Man On His Back. Without hesitation, the elder replied that it was so named by "the people" when, a long time ago, "we found an old man up there, in bad shape."

It was as if the proverbial anvil had fallen out of the sky. I realized, with much dismay at my own typically non-Amerindian blindness, that of course such a name had to be Amerindian, for I knew perfectly well that although we almost never name land features in that way, Amerindians typically do. It was certainly not the first time I'd failed to understand or, worse, even to acknowledge the First Nations' point of view about the world.

Despite paying lip service to the understanding that all this land had belonged once to Amerindian people, I had failed to have a sense of that as something real and practical and everyday—real people, real land that they walked on and rode their horses on, and were born and died on, and knew and understood, and had given names to, and had loved and revered as the great gift to them from their Creator. Then it hit me, with the force of true comprehension at last, what we had done when we settlers had claimed this land for our own.

At the inaugural ceremonies held on a high hill on the Old Man On His Back Prairie and Heritage Preserve, the elder said to me, "I had a dream." I moved closer to him, eager to hear it and deeply honoured that he would tell me. "I dreamt the people were all around," he said, gesturing to the hills and fields of grass and blooming wildflowers stretching out all around us, "and they were happy."

Chapter 6

STONES AND BONES

ONE EARLY SPRING DAY WHEN THERE WAS STILL SNOW IN the coulees and sheltered spots and running water from snow melt elsewhere, I was out picking my way carefully through the field. At the bottom of a deep coulee I found something that looked like bone, very large, and mostly still submerged in the wet, slick clay. What protruded above the ground, knee-high on me, washed clear of earth by the spring runoff, could have been the hip bone of a large animal, even to the opening where the leg would have fitted into the socket. It was stained a brownish colour from the minerals in the soil and running water, but it was hard, like rock, and clearly too big to be the bone of a cow or a horse. My heart speeded up when I saw it, and as I crouched by it, moving around it, touching it in rising excitement, I thought that I had found a fossilized dinosaur skeleton.

It surprises me now how difficult it was to find the right person to tell this story to, but eventually, at least a year later, I drove into town to meet a paleontologist at Jack's Café, and together we drove out to the nearest road to the field and then walked into the coulee. He saw the hip bone from a distance, and pausing in his walking to survey the high coulee wall, he remarked casually that the location was likely for fossil finds because the washing-away effect over the centuries that had produced the coulee had bared the earth to the Cretaceous level, that is, to the level where the dinosaurs once walked. We walked on in silence. At the bone, he walked around it, studied it from every angle, then crouching, reached into the capacious pocket of his grey canvas field jacket and took out a small, silver-headed hammer.

I'm sure my eyes widened. I swear a bead or two of perspiration appeared on his brow, perhaps in that instant's hesitation he even said a small prayer, and then with one swift, clean blow of his hammer, he broke off a small piece of the bone. He held the chunk up to the light and examined it, and then he said, without discernible emotion, "What you have here is a concretion."

"A what?" I said. He explained, showing me the clean surface revealed by the break. If this had been bone, he explained, you'd see marrow here. But this is just a strange shape in the soil caused by erosion. "We find them all the time, and they fool us too." If he was disappointed, he didn't show it, but again, when we were about to walk away, he paused to stare back up at the coulee wall and then to look carefully at the landscape in each direction. I wondered if he was mentally marking the site for further investigation some day.

Then one summer day in 1994 Peter and I drove into town, and on one street corner the amplifier from a tape player sat on the steps of a store broadcasting loudly what sounded to me like bird noises: squawks, bleats, and chirps. On the opposite corner, another storefront had been transformed by the addition of long, wide banners proclaiming, in foot-high, bright-red print, "Souvenirs." Most of the shop windows in the town had murals painted on them in bright primary colours which, on closer examination, turned out to be depictions of a large green creature standing on his rear legs performing everyday household tasks, wearing a grin that hovered between fiendish and drunken. When we tried to park near the store where we wanted to shop, we couldn't—astonishingly, all the parking places were taken. And there were strangers strolling the streets everywhere, and the parked vehicles carried licence plates from all over North America.

Somebody said to me in the following days, "I think you predicted this!" It was a joke, but in *The Fourth Archangel*, a novel I published in 1992, I did draw just such a scenario. The town in my novel had filled with strangers, transforming it, because one of the local teenage girls claimed to have received the stigmata, although whether she was merely a hysteric, a liar, or the real thing is never made clear. Now here it was, before our startled eyes, although I noted that none of the crowds of people were on their knees praying aloud in the streets, nor were any hymns being sung. The strangers, contrary to those in my novel, were a healthy-looking lot, suntanned and clad in shorts, T-shirts, wearing Tilley hats and hiking boots and driving expensive vehicles.

What had happened was that Tim Tokaryk, the paleontologist who had come out to the field with me that day and used his hammer to show me I had found only a concretion, John Storer, the curator of Earth Sciences at the Royal Saskatchewan Museum in Regina, and Robert Gebhardt, the local high school principal, while out fossil prospecting on August 16, 1991, only a few miles down the valley from our house, had found the fossilized bones of a *Tyrannosaurus rex*. (It was Gebhardt who first spotted a tooth but who wasn't able to identify it, and the other two who confirmed what he'd found and, digging around in the loose dirt, found more.) It was a major find, at that time only the twelfth in the world, only five of which were relatively complete as this one was suspected of being, and the first found in Saskatchewan.

They kept it a secret—at that time they were the only paleontologists in the province—until they'd completed other excavation work they had elsewhere, and finally, in spring 1994, as the saying goes, "all hell broke loose," when we woke to the thrilling news being proclaimed around the world, and the excavation of the fossil began at last.

If it was the kind of find that paleontologists dream all their lives of making, it was also the dream of the merchants of small-town Saskatchewan. The rural and small-town population of the province had peaked some time in the twenties and ever since had been falling off, at first gradually and then more rapidly, until in the eighties and nineties with the closing of small, local elevators and the shutting down of branchline railways all over the province, town after town was facing its imminent commercial demise, which nearly always means its demise in every other way too.

Many, if not most, prairie towns had been established by the railway early in the twentieth century, usually about nine miles apart along the rail line, since nine miles was about as far as a farmer could make a round trip in one day hauling grain by horse and wagon. Whether there was water, a pleasant view, shelter, or any other natural amenity for the settlers was not a consideration. Consequently, once the grain elevator and the branch railway were dismantled, there was nothing left to hold people, resulting in the disappearance of many villages established early in this century.

Eastend, however, was set in the Frenchman River valley with high hills and cliffs all around it, with a narrow, pretty river encircling it, providing a water supply, pleasant picnic sites, and constant excitement for children growing up on its banks. Its deep wooded coulees and draws held a clean water supply and gave shelter to wild animals and were good places for humans to winter safe from the ravages of wind and bitter cold on the open prairie. For a very long time, before there was a province, or a store, or a farmer, there had been people living in the area (as the stone artifacts everywhere the land is unploughed had demonstrated), or traversing it regularly in hunting and berry-picking parties. Archeological digs revealed what had long been known to be in Chimney Coulee where the town had begun: a Hudson's Bay Company post, the Northwest Mounted Police post, as well as the remains of the houses of Métis winterers. We all felt that Eastend would have survived the loss of its elevators and railway branchline, although probably in an abbreviated form.

The discovery of the T-rex (or Mr. T-rex, as people liked to refer to the creature, although its gender is unknown) would save Eastend from slipping backward into an existence as just another dead-end prairie hamlet. Thus, when Peter and I drove into town that hot summer day, we were confronted with the first signs of new commercial enterprise in a place which had barely changed in years and which had always been isolated and quiet, so far off the beaten track that few tourists ever came near it.

The T-rex was far from the first fossil find in the area. Residents who knew of it would joke that Regina's Royal Saskatchewan Museum's Earth Sciences wing would have to close if all the fossils from the Eastend area were taken away. Fossils had been shipped to the Royal Ontario Museum in Toronto and elsewhere around the world as well. At the site where the T-rex was being excavated by Tim Tokaryk and his crew, so many other finds were made, as those workers camping on the site (at "Camp Cow Patty") wandered the cliffs and draws in the evening, that Tim, for the time being, had to forbid any further prospecting, since they already had far more work than their small crew could handle.

Fossil collecting had begun with an Englishman named Harold S. ("Corky") Jones (1880–1978), who had come to Western Canada at eighteen to be a cowboy and begun his career working for one of the big ranches near Eastend. Although he had no higher education, he became interested in collecting and to that end developed a relationship with C. M. Sternberg of the Canadian Museum of Nature in Ottawa. To this day many of his finds can be seen in the local museum on the mainstreet of Eastend, expanded by more recent finds, including the partial skull of a triceratops, the shield of torosaurus, and the full skeleton of a brontothere (a mere 37-million-year-old mammal—not a dinosaur).

Local business people and the town's leaders lobbied the provincial government hard to keep the T-rex in Eastend instead of shipping it off to Regina or even farther afield, and for once their efforts were fruitful. There has been a Fossil Research Field Station in Eastend managed by Tim Tokaryk since 1994, and in the spring of 1999, work began on a major dinosaur interpretive centre, expected to cost $3.1 million, designed to link to, instead of compete with, the Tyrrell Museum of Paleontology at Drumheller, Alberta. The new interpretive centre will bring permanent jobs, a steady flow of tourists, and be the source of a reasonably stable economic base for an area otherwise dependent on the increasingly unpredictable fortunes of agriculture.

Nobody expected that Eastend would swell to city size or that there'd be more jobs than people, but the future looked brighter for the town than it had since 1914 when it was first established. This was, incidentally, the same spring that Wallace Stegner arrived with his mother, brother, and "boomer" father, who followed the frontier, dragging his family with him, in hopes of making his fortune at the edge of civilization. So far the only fortune produced for the

Stegners by Eastend had been Wallace's very successful and remarkable book about the town called *Wolf Willow: A History, a Story, and a Memory of the Last Plains Frontier*, published in 1962.

As Tim had already explained to me, the Eastend area is a rich source of fossils from the age of the dinosaurs because the glaciers, which here melted back about twelve thousand years ago, had in many places scraped the earth down to that of the Cretaceous period (from about 144 million to 65 million years ago), exposing at or near the surface the fossilized bones which elsewhere on earth are buried beneath tons of earth. The various layers of earth that one can see with the naked eye in many places along the Frenchman River are (explained to me by Tim Tokaryk) "local stratigraphic units—types of sediment that fit into a grander bracket of geological time." These are chiefly the Ravenscrag Formation, the White Mud Formation, and the Frenchman Formation.

John Storer says that the Frenchman Formation, which represents the last 1.5 million years of the Cretaceous period, preserves what may be Canada's finest record of the end of the Mesozoic era, the "Age of Dinosaurs." The Mesozoic era, containing the Triassic, Jurassic, and Cretaceous periods, was a time, according to Storer, when continental drift took place, moving our area from warmer climates to cooler ones, and when the sea which covered what became Saskatchewan finally withdrew, forests grew, and many animals, including dinosaurs, inhabited them.

"You have to understand," he told a gathering of writers attending the Writing the Land Conference organized by the local arts council in Eastend in July 1994, "that there was no *there* then." By this he meant that when our T-rex died, it was not just that there was no Eastend, no rural municipality, but that there was no America; the continents during Cretaceous times were a different shape, and the climate was like that of present-day Southeast Asia, along with similar flora. Even a zealous researcher, studying John Storer's *Geological History of Saskatchewan*, trying to find a reference point between *then* and *now*, gives up in despair. There is none, not familiar mountains, lakes, or rivers, not even latitude, since when the T-rex died in its streambed (hence, the jumble of bones the paleontologists found instead of a neatly laid-out skeleton), the location was farther north.

Tim also pointed out in an article published in *Geology Today* that "the last seventy-five million years are preserved in this region in relative completeness—late Cretaceous marine and non-marine faunas, Paleocene through to Miocene terrestrial faunas, and a few scattered deposits from the Quaternary," each of these periods bringing us closer to the present day. In other words, the Eastend area is a gold mine of fossils covering a wide range of geological eras.

If it is nearly impossible to understand the flux of the earth's surface over the millions of years since its genesis—humanless, animal-less, plantless—it is also very hard for a mere human being in the twenty-first century to really understand that *Tyrannosaurus rex* existed, walked the earth as we do today, called this planet home. All of this exists for us more in the realm of the mythical than the scientific or the "real."

In trying to convince oneself of the reality of such a creature, it doesn't help that the animal itself was so large and so frightening. He stood up to 6 metres (20 feet) tall at the hip, was 13.5 to 15 metres (45 to 50 feet) long, and weighed up to 6.4 tonnes (7 tons). If its row of sixty 15-to-20-centimetre (6-to-8-inch) dagger-like teeth aren't enough to terrify, the animal, on the evidence of the bone structure of its legs, probably ran 70 to 80 kilometres per hour (40 to 50 miles per hour). Somebody has described it as "the roadrunner from hell." It was, of course, a flesh-eater, although it had no chewing mechanism and tore flesh instead. Its massive head was balanced by a long, heavy tail. While its powerful back legs ended in 20-centimetre (8-inch) talons, its arms were, in one of the major puzzles about it, only about 76 centimetres (30 inches) long, too short for it even to scratch its own chin. No one has come up with a reasonable explanation for this. As Tim explained, surprisingly little is known about the *Tyrannosaurus rex*, in part because it was a large carnivore, and large carnivores, even today, are present in far fewer numbers than plant-eaters, making them relatively rare.

The first T-rex was found only in 1900 in Wyoming by Barnard Brown, a great fossil hunter working for the American Museum of Natural History. By the time Eastend's T-rex was found, twelve in all had been discovered, one in Wyoming, five in Montana, three in South Dakota, and two in Alberta. In the five years that followed Eastend's excavation, a number more have been found in the same areas of the continent as the first twelve, but it's rumoured that some finds are being kept secret because of a dispute that erupted over ownership of the one found in South Dakota in 1990 (called "Sue"), which was the most complete at about 90 per cent and was then also the largest.

The quarrel was between the fossil collector and the owner of the land on which the fossil had been found. When this quarrel could not be resolved amicably, the FBI impounded the fossil, and finally, in a highly publicized court case, a judge gave ownership to the rancher who'd given the fossil collector permission to search on his land. Then "Sue" went on the auction block at Sothebys the fall of 1997, and the Field Museum of Chicago bought it for eight million dollars. What happened with "Sue," unfortunately, has made collectors even more secretive about their finds.

The delight of the Eastend's merchants and leaders over the discovery wasn't in error. Over the summer, close to twelve thousand people from as far away as Korea and Japan visited, of whom over six thousand took the official site tour. And while tourists brought about $800,000 to Eastend, they also spent some $2.5 million in southwest Saskatchewan over the summer. Nearby Pine Cree Park, the much larger Cypress Hills Park, even motels in Swift Current, ninety miles northeast on the Trans-Canada Highway, reported an increase in business from tourists on their way to or from Eastend's dinosaur dig. If the town leaders' gratification was well founded in commercial terms, I at least felt that, as the sole public reaction, something was wrong, or if not exactly wrong, something was missing, something wasn't being said that needed to be said, although just what it was, I wasn't sure.

For most people in Eastend, though, those not running businesses—the many retired farmers and ranchers, the schoolteachers, the clergy, those selling items not needed by tourists such as farm supplies—the discovery of the fossil meant only having to deal with traffic or not being able to find a place to park or a seat in the café. Careful records were kept of the addresses of those who took the bus tours to the paleontology dig, showing that only 7 per cent of them were from this area—the rest were tourists—and that the number with local addresses comprised a surprising mere 7 per cent of the area population.

One day as I was sitting in the doctor's waiting room, the conversation got around, as it always did in those first, exciting days, to Mr. T-rex. A sixtyish gentleman said in a disgruntled, stubborn way,

"How do they know it's sixty-five million years old? I don't believe it. I think they made it up."

I was surprised by this remark, or maybe amused would be a better word. But I thought also that it meant that finally somebody cared about the meaning, the significance of finding a dinosaur, that this man lay awake at night puzzling over it as I was doing, that he wished somebody would make sense of it for him because it was more than he could do for himself, and a part of him was baffled and stunned. He recognized, I thought, that here was a great mystery, and all the explanations in the world from the scientists told him nothing of what he really wanted to know, although what that was he couldn't exactly articulate.

Then I remembered that southwest Saskatchewan has a dispro-portionately large number of fundamentalist churches, from Plymouth Brethren to Church of God. There'd been attempts made to stop the teaching of dinosaurs in schools in at least one nearby town, and later the same churchgoers had fought, this time successfully, to get rid of all games in the school with witches and dragons. In fact, I was told by local people that on one occasion families belonging to one of these churches had dressed in their best and stayed up all night in their church waiting for the world to end. (I was so fascinated by this that I went in search of books about such phenomena. It appears that when such groups find their prediction fails to come true, they don't consider that perhaps they were wrong in the first place, that maybe they are simply not privy to special information about the ending of the world; instead, they simply change the date.) But now I wondered what the members of the large body of fundamentalist churches were making of the find. Did they simply refuse to accept that there was a dinosaur and that it was sixty-five million years old?

I'd been hired to write a magazine article about the effect of the discovery on the town, and this gave me an excuse to ask questions of people I wouldn't otherwise have spoken to. I went to the church members and their pastors about the discovery. I was told that since most of them believed in Bishop Usher's dating of the earth as about ten thousand years old, as I'd expected, either the dinosaurs had to be discounted completely or else a way had to be devised to include them in their churches' version of creation. One pastor told me, "We believe that dinosaurs went on the ark too—all the creatures were small so as to be accommodated—and that dinosaurs came off the ark but died soon because the geology and vegetation had changed. Fossils were created when those not on the ark were instantly compressed by the weight of the floodwaters." This explanation struck me as a rather outlandish response to what I thought was the incontrovertible evidence before all of us if we cared to look.

But when it comes right down to it, it seemed to me, too, that the town's response, instantly to see the dinosaur as a major marketing opportunity, although a lot more predictable, wasn't much more profound in terms of the meaning, or layers of meaning, of the discovery. If the explanation of the fundamentalist pastors surprised me as much as the old gentleman's remark in the doctor's office, I was still no closer to finding a place to put the dinosaur in my own scheme of creation.

But Tim Tokaryk, chatting with me at the dig that fall, said he'd been having wonderful dreams "about evolution and miraculous things happening." When Tim told me this, for an instant, I caught my breath because at last somebody had said something that gave me a glimpse of the profundity, the scale of the world this placed not only our dinosaur in, but our village, our very homes, our own lives.

But Tim was hard at work in the quarry in plus-100-degree temperatures all day, every day, and in no position to spend time pursuing this line of thought for my edification. I went then to my friend Greg Grace, a published poet and, at the time, Eastend's United Church minister, in hopes that he would have the resources to say what I couldn't say, to part the veil of hard scientific fact and the myths of one sort or another surrounding the creature. Greg said he needed a day or so to think about it, so we planned to meet for lunch later in the week.

When we finally did, I wasn't disappointed. Greg began by pointing out that the dragon is central to English literature. He mentioned *Beowulf* (the first extant work of English literature), which is about the slaying of a dragon, the story of St. George and the dragon, Spenser's *The Faerie Queen* about huge demonic forces, and the dragon in the Book of Revelation representing Babylon—as he put it, "a self-indulgent consuming society. So the dragon is also an image of who we are in a negative sense. It represents the reptilian in us, the dark side we tend to repress. But," he went on, "there's also a nobility, something to respect about it. It's ancient, alien, and dangerous, but it has a power that's beyond us. It threatens our comfortable perspectives and throws us into a kind of chaos."

The merchants' response to the discovery, he said, had to do with the T-rex as "a real image of horror—all teeth, a flesh-eating machine—the ultimate consumer." We both laughed at this. "Domesticated, reduced to a cartoon on a T-shirt, the power is lost, although the fascination remains." Imagining him living amongst us, as humans seem to be unable to avoid doing as we struggle to grasp his reality, inevitably evokes terror and dread of a magnitude with which we simply cannot cope.

In other words, the coffee mugs with dinosaurs painted on the side for sale in town, the two-inch-long children's toy dinosaurs, the cuddly stuffed dinosaurs, the children's dinosaur-shaped birthday cake pans, and the cheerful, domesticated T-rex painted on the stores' windows turned the T-rex into a joke, rendered him harmless, reduced him to something emotionally manageable.

Greg was dead-on, I thought, and although I came away genuinely enlightened from our conversation, I still felt that there was a greater mystery not resolved, not yet touched upon in any but scientific terms: This is how it happened, and this is how we know it happened. It was an answer of a kind, but it made me feel the helpless school kid again in a science class, begging her teacher to answer her question which was always, "But why?" until he got furious, since the only "why" he could answer had to do with equations and formulas and evidence before his eyes. For him, it seemed to me, there never was any further 'why.' What he had was sufficient, while his answers told me nothing, and as a child, I could only conclude I must be a moron.

I went to the dig three times, and I saw that the field where the quarry was looks a lot like the field where I go for walks and where I once thought I'd found a fossil myself. Someone had told me that, more than a hundred miles to the west of us, a party of paleontologists scouted that area all one summer without any success. At last they gave up, packed up their camp and their equipment, and loaded their vehicles for departure. But as they drove away, one member of the party turned and looked back. There he saw, gleaming out from the valley wall, the full skeleton of a dinosaur. I remembered how, as we walked away from the concretion I'd found, Tim had paused and looked back, gazing carefully up and down the coulee walls, before he'd turned back to face the trail out.

The day I saw what looked to be a dinosaur bone, I knew none of this, and when I gradually began to know it, I found myself looking at the field with new eyes, trying but failing to grasp in any even faintly satisfactory way what this meant about a few acres of land for which Peter held a deed and which all of us thought of in terms of its potential, or lack of, for agriculture. I imagined the earth, a great stone hurtling through space at a speed beyond the ability of the imagination to grasp—a ball endlessly spinning as it flies, even as I kneel, examining a perfect yellow violet no bigger than my smallest fingernail, or hold up a stone sphere and a cylinder, puzzling over them, then consign them back to the place I found them.

Now it struck me with the force of a revelation: I was walking on dinosaurs. Beneath my feet, everywhere I walked in my home country, I walked on the past. Not just the archeological past but the paleontological past, the past so remote it is beyond understanding, so remote it is refused understanding by nearly everyone, so remote it can be conceived of only by making an enormous leap of understanding, or perhaps of faith, over those millions of years of time between now and then. It meant that, in some dizzying way, the coulee where I found what I thought was a sixty-five-million-year-old dinosaur bone turned to stone was at once both place and time.

I pondered this, barely able to grasp it. Looking up and down the field to the high places and the low places, to the places where there was a natural scatter of stones and the places where there were none, trying to understand what it was, what its nature was, I remembered my third year in university when I was forced into taking a geography class, since it was that or math or no degree. It was a survey class, and we did units on climatology, historical geography, economic geography, and physical geography, which involved some geology. Up to that time I'd no perception of the world as making sense, as fitting together in some coherent way, as one thing following another with a degree of rationality. It all just *was*, and what I learned in this class was a great revelation to me, and one which, nearly forty years later, after most of the facts had long since abandoned me, I still cherished, for it had changed the way I viewed the world.

I knew the glaciers had designed the field the way it was. Crunching and grinding, as they'd expanded and then retreated, they had somehow brought rocks here from as far away as the Rocky Mountains to the west, I'd heard, and from the Canadian Shield far to the north and east. One of the things that had always fascinated me about the field was the great variety, in terms of texture and colour more even than size, of the rocks. They varied from some soft ones that looked as if a painter had rolled them with a fashionable tan colour and left them out to dry, to boulders of glittering pink or grey granite, to small flat rocks so full of mica flecks that in the summer sun they shone like pools of water, to the rare ugly brownish black stone that someone walking the field with me said looked like uranium-bearing ore. There were stones of pure white quartz of varying sizes, and golden chert, and solid black rocks of different types—some were the finest-grained granite, and some others looked more vitreous and shiny, the largest of which was probably basalt, while others were a dull, flat black belonging to no category I could name. There were the most beautiful small rose-red stones, sandstone, and everywhere softer stones, from simple solidified mud to those with a harder texture that were often pale beige but that sometimes were flushed with pink and mauve. I'd once been a painter, I loved colour, and I came to love the stones for their simple, colourful, surprising beauty. I wondered if it was normal, average, for there to be so many different types—sedimentary, igneous, metamorphic—all lying side by side or on top of each other in the same field. I decided that this, too, must be the result of glacial retreating and advancing.

Some of the stones were so old and weathered they looked more like plants than rock; usually they were coated with growths of lichen, some close to half an inch thick, lichen growing on lichen, green on grey, or charcoal on cream. One pink granite rock on the bottom of a former watercourse was worn by the water's rushing over it till it was as smooth as a cushion someone had just been sitting on. Some rocks were concave in places, as if a sculptor had carved out the interior and then polished it smooth, and others were cracked, some so deeply that they'd split apart and lay like the Sunday roast, in neat slices side by side. Others had become a cascade of beige chips and flakes scattered down an earthen hillside of nearly the same colour, on their way to becoming earth again. Some were flat, tipped on their sides, or with chipped and pitted surfaces so that I studied them closely on the off chance they might be petroglyphs, which would be a really important find. They lay in clusters or scatters, reminding me of walruses or frogs or great crustaceans up from the bottom of the primal sea, many-layered, coated and peeling and grooved, all sharp lines and angles long since worn away.

And they were different sizes. The biggest boulder, granite, had the indentation in the earth around its base that prairie people recognize immediately as caused by the tramping of animals using the stone to scratch itches and to chase away insects; and the polished, shiny spots caused by the rubbing—a buffalo rubbing stone, which, since the demise of the buffalo in the 1880s, would have been used by range cattle. There were lots of tiny chips that gradually became sandy patches, and a few spots which were gravel. Fairly often I'd come across smooth, somewhat flattened, ovoid stones usually of chert and about the size of a half-loaf of bread which people here call cobblestones. Someone told me the grinding action of the glaciers had worn such stones to their smoothness and perfect shape and was also responsible for the scatter of half-moon grooves on the ends.

For some reason—the glaciers again, I guessed—the stones were strewn down the ridges and in the lower place where there'd once been a watercourse and now in which the spring runoff and any heavy rains ran down. In the central basin there were almost no stones at all, but as I walked the hills and the draws, I often came upon stones scattered about or lying in piles so old that grass and earth had grown around them, and I could not explain how they'd arrived there. But neither did I worry much about it. I had developed a kind of faith that what was required of me was that I walk and look and think, changing nothing, moving nothing, and some day I would know whatever it was I needed to know.

But the discovery of the dinosaur, and the one I thought I'd found here in the field, had opened a new dimension in my brain, a kind of hollowed-out place that was vast and ended somewhere in the stars and with the Big Bang when this earth had been formed. I would stop and stand and stare up at the hillsides, and they, the grass, the stones, the patches of clay, would positively gleam at me with light that seemed more internal than external and from the sun, and I would know that they were filled with spirit too. And I pondered that, and pondered it.

And I knew that where I stood was once an immense river: a place in the field we would call a draw, with a floor of rocks and gravel that was easy to see as riverbottom. Each year this place eroded a little deeper with the snowmelt. One day it could easily erode to the level of the dinosaurs or, eventually, long after I was dead and buried, maybe even deeper than that, through bones and many more layers of rocks, until at last it reached down into the earth's fiery centre and, thus, to the beginning of time.

Heart

Chapter 7

CAIRNS

IN THE EARLY NINETIES THE SASKATCHEWAN WRITERS guild staged its annual conference in Regina, and I was to take part in a panel on rural life. My presentation was a near-disaster because I had more material than I could handle or even make much sense of in such a short time. That material developed into *The Perfection of the Morning*, and I wasn't well enough organized that afternoon because I was still sorting my way intellectually and emotionally through it and couldn't condense it yet despite a considerable effort.

But I had spoken about matters usually reserved for Amerindian lecturers: animals on the land and how one recognizes them—by the shape of their heads, by the way they move; the feeling one gets when imagining a life lived in a tepee *on* the ground instead of several feet above it and insulated by many layers of material; and other such matters. I was trying to talk about what I had learned about living in Nature. I did not speak about these things as one who knows them but as one who was taking her first faltering steps in their directions, as one who was beginning to ask appropriate questions about a life lived *on the ground*, as Amerindian people live it or, at least within living memory, used to.

I said from the stage to the one Amerindian person in the audience, a Cree woman I knew slightly, "I hope I haven't offended." When the panel ended and members of the audience came up to the platform to speak with those of us on the stage, she came too and stood at the back of the small group until anyone who wanted to speak to us had done so. Then she held out her hand to me, palm down, fist closed. Hesitantly, I put out my hand to accept whatever it was. She let it drop into my palm.

It was a stone, an oval-shaped brown stone striped in concentric narrow black bands, about an inch at its widest part and an inch and a quarter long. She said clearly, quietly, as she gave it to me, "You haven't offended."

I had no idea what this meant, although I could see it was something good. I thanked her, and I said, "When we meet again, I'll have one for you." She looked taken aback, and I guessed that I'd failed to understand the gesture (which was true) and had responded in an inappropriate way. Then she went away. I can't recall ever having seen her again, although I know she has since moved to another province and is not a phantom.

I pondered that gift idly for years and one day thought to ask a specialist in Plains archeology if he knew what it meant. "Hmmm," he said, "really," and it was clear he was both surprised and impressed, that the gesture was not one that Amerindian people made to non-Amerindians often. "Stones are sacred," I believe he said, not looking at me, or "Stones can be sacred," and left it at that.

I know stones have power. Having seen on television the newly discovered sundial at Chaco Canyon thought to track the solstices, equinoxes, and the nineteen-year phases of the moon, when Peter and I were planning our trip to New Mexico some years ago, I had an idea. I thought I'd take a stone from the centre of a certain small stone circle to a site of similar importance in New Mexico. I suppose I was thinking of something in Chaco Canyon, perhaps a kiva, and that from there I would collect a stone in return and place it in the centre of the same small circle at home. I've no idea why I wanted to do this or what I thought would be accomplished by it. But I chose a small piece lying on the surface of a sandstone rock from which it had been broken by frost, put it in the pocket of my jeans, and went smugly away.

Arriving in New Mexico, we rented a car and began to drive to interesting sites in the northwest corner of the state. It was February, a fairly high elevation and surprisingly colder here than it was at that moment at our Saskatchewan home. We were chagrined to learn that we couldn't get into Chaco Canyon because a heavy snowfall had melted and made the last twenty or so unpaved miles into the Canyon impassable to all but four-wheel drives. Our little rent-a-car with its thirteen-inch wheels would never make it. Ah, well. We drove on.

At another site, an ancient Anasazi village developed as a tourist site, we were the only visitors; even the site operator was not to be found. There were signs forbidding absolutely entry into any of the kivas—round ceremonial rooms dug into the ground, but missing the upper walls and ceilings they would originally have had—but understanding them as sacred places, we wouldn't have dreamt of it anyway. Explanatory signs had been installed, and there were crushed stone paths among the various representatives of the homes in which Amerindians of the area had lived in ancient times.

I carried the stone I had taken from Saskatchewan in my pocket, where it had been since early that morning. It was hot to touch, I thought, from hours of lying with only a thin cloth between it and my flesh, and as I put my hand in my pocket to extract it, I felt such resistance, which I read as my own—that I didn't want to throw the stone into a kiva, that I wanted to keep it—that I almost didn't. But I lectured myself: You came all this way, you brought the stone with you, think how much you'll regret not having done what you set out to do. I took it from my pocket and tossed it into a kiva.

The neat paths among the kivas weren't made of gravel as I know it, but of some other, porous, lightweight, beige-coloured stone, and it was clear they'd been built when the site was opened to tourists and weren't of ancient origin. If I couldn't get a stone from a kiva, where was I to get one to carry back to place in the stone circle at home? I could see no other place, so finally, exasperated as I saw my plan disintegrating, I picked one from the path and put it in my pocket. We drove on, heading towards Taos in search of dinner and a bed for the night.

Then I began to feel ill. I am prone to car sickness, but if I'm not riding in fog and I'm in the front seat, I'm never bothered. I told Peter I was feeling sick, and we considered that it might be from the altitude, although I'd never suffered from altitude sickness before in the Rockies or the Kootenays, and when later that week we went up to ten thousand feet outside Albuquerque and stayed there long enough to have dinner, I was fine, if terrified, in the gondola going up. Nor did I suffer from altitude sickness years later when travelling for days, over eight thousand feet, in Ethiopia.

My nausea kept getting worse, until I was leaning back in the seat, my eyes closed, fighting not to give in to it. We arrived at a snow-covered mountain pass, Peter pulled over, stopped the car, and got out to look at the view. I was too ill to move, but I did roll down the window in hope that the cold air would help me.

Then I thought, *It's the stone; I shouldn't have taken the stone.* It was still there, pressing against my leg in the pocket of my jeans. I pushed my hand into my pocket, retrieved the stone I'd taken from the path, and threw it out into the pass. Peter heard the sound of it striking snow and turned to see what it was, but said nothing. I didn't explain, and he got back in the car and we drove on.

At the moment I tossed the stone out the window I felt a heavy weight I hadn't known was there lift off my shoulders, and I leaned back, relieved, thinking now I would be fine, since obviously I'd been right—there'd been a curse put on anybody who stole anything from the site.

But it didn't make any difference. Even though I was somewhat better, I still felt ill. That night in Taos I had to go straight to bed, and Peter had to go out for dinner by himself. Before he left, since I was unable to eat anything, he brought me a Coke, but when I sipped it, the small amount I'd swallowed immediately reversed direction, came back up, and believe it or not, foamed up out my nose, a new and not terribly fun experience. Okay, I said, I learned my lesson. The next day I was fine, if a bit shaky.

I say, casually, that someone "put a curse" on the stone, although of course I don't know that. I might just as easily have said that the stone didn't want to come with me and was exerting what influence it could to make me not want to carry it any farther, although I don't know that either. If I hadn't felt a weight lift from my shoulders when I threw the stone away, I'd probably just say I'd developed a flu—if I didn't already strongly suspect that stones have power, if I didn't know that traditional Amerindian people have always known of the power inherent in stone. My experiences in the field had provided a foundation for fully accepting such a belief system whether, as a late-twentieth-century North American with European ancestors, raised as a Christian, I could partake of it myself or not. I had not yet had my strange experience with the stone circle on Fair Isle, but when I did, it helped to confirm my growing awareness of stones as representing something powerful, or being in themselves powerful.

I had always meant to climb to the highest point of the field at the end farthest from where I entered the field. But the field was so invariably fascinating, and I was suffering from this strange tiredness, that nearly every time I went there, by the time I was anywhere near that end of the field, I was too tired to climb the hundred or more feet to that very high point.

The reason I was interested in going there was that from a distance it was possible to see a faint bump on the horizon where the line of the hills met the sky. This bump, I knew, would be a pile of stones. I thought, most of the time anyway, that the pile would have been put there by a farmer when he was clearing his field of stones in preparation for ploughing it, but I couldn't be sure until I'd seen it. Years passed before, finally, one day I made the climb up to it.

I believe when I first saw it, I hesitated over my suspicion that it was merely a farmer's rock pile, because it was clear that the field on which it sat had never been ploughed, nor had the field next to it. It occurred to me that possibly a farmer had cleared the stones intending to plough the field, but then hadn't done so.

But the more I studied the pile of rocks, the more it seemed to me that no farmer had piled it. It was waist-high on a man, covering a diameter of perhaps ten or twelve feet, and studying the formation closely, I could see that the bottom layers of the rocks were partly embedded in the prairie and that nearly all of them had a coat of lichen, the lowest ones having very thick coats. Further, as I walked around it, it seemed to me that there might once have been a thick outer circle of stones, perhaps three feet from what had been the periphery of the large central pile, or if not, these stones might have been knocked from the top. I looked more carefully, and now I saw that to one side of the great stone cairn there was an area of stones embedded in the earth, as if a second cairn had once been there. I was sure I was looking at a cairn made by Amerindians at some time in the last twelve thousand years, and now I wanted to know what this was, what it was for, if it was *for* anything.

In one of my books I found an undated photograph of the Bracken Cairn Site (Bracken is a small community near Eastend). In the photograph, the cairn looked just like a smaller version of the cairn I was looking at, and it was in a similar location, that is, on a high point with an unobstructed view for miles in three directions.

The author reported that the Bracken Cairn had been excavated in 1948 by a sister and brother using only a penknife and a screw-driver—the pit was only four feet deep—and that they had found, in addition to some grave goods, two bundles of human bones, "each with a skull facing west." The Saskatchewan Museum of Natural History (now the Royal Saskatchewan Museum) became involved in 1957, but it wasn't until 1981 that a complete analysis of the bones was done by an archeologist.

The site was radiocarbon-dated to about twenty-five hundred years ago, the people (the bones were the remains of five individuals, including two children, one a newborn and one about a year old, all stained with red ochre) were designated as belonging to the Pelican Lake culture, which had appeared on the Plains about thirty-three hundred years ago. Among the grave goods were two gorgets—pendants—made of clam shell native to the Gulf of Mexico. Now I thought I had a rough idea of this cairn's date, as well as the startling fact that there would almost certainly be human bones beneath the stones and a shallow layer of earth. I was looking at a grave.

The cairn made me want to know more about the system of belief, the religion of the people who'd built it, in order to understand its meaning. Was this perhaps ancestor worship? I went to my books, where I found that anthropologists don't classify the practice of veneration of the worthy dead among Amerindians as true ancestor worship such as it is practised in Africa and Asia. Among Amerindians, my books said, respect for one's ancestors was an aspect but wasn't the most important or motivating part of their religion. Still, I was looking at a grave, one that had taken some time and effort to make, and when I could add nothing to my barest understanding of it, I thought about the site not too far away, which earlier in this book I'd called, tentatively, a vision-quest site—a small circle of stone, but no cairn—and how I had fled from it.

I realized now that the stone circle was a holy place which I had desecrated by so casually stepping into the circle. So when I found the high mound of stones on the highest point with the widest view to be a burial cairn, I began at last to put the proverbial two and two together. Something important was going on here—something *had* gone on here in the field, or the field *was* something—and I wanted to know what it was.

I asked a passing archeologist about another enigmatic pile of large rocks which I kept noticing as I walked about in the field. It was a short way up the rising edge of one end of the central basin area. It's actually a scatter of stone, and when I examined it closely, I saw that at two points there seemed to be several layers of rocks, while the remainder appeared to be resting directly on the ground. The whole area of stone scatter is perhaps twenty feet in the north-south and east-west directions, but it isn't round, and the stones vary in size, with the largest encrusted with lichen, signifying that they hadn't been dug up out of the earth, at least, not recently.

Viewed from the northwest you see only one hip-high boulder, but from the south and east you see what appears to be a pile of stones, which turns into a scatter of rocks when you get close to it.

The archeologist remarked, after a cursory look, that it was probably piled by farmers, and although I wasn't quite convinced, for a long time I left it at that because I knew there had been an early settler who'd had a shack and a dugout barn on the edge of the field not far from this pile of stones. He'd been there around 1910, when the first wave of settlers had come to this area, and he hadn't stayed long at this site. There was no trace of a building left, only the disturbed earth on the south-facing slope of a low hill at the boundary of the field, and farther on, in the next field, a grass-covered cellar hole.

But, almost certainly being poor and with tractors not being readily available yet, he wouldn't have had a tractor to move the rocks, and as far as we could tell, neither the field nor the one below it had ever been ploughed. Most of the rocks, at about thirty inches by eighteen inches and a foot to two feet deep, were too big for one person to carry by himself, and there seemed to be no reason in the first place to do so, since no settler—a way of life defined by its unrelenting, unavoidable hard work merely to stay alive—in his right mind would make unnecessary work for himself. Nor did it make sense to think that the retreating glaciers might have dropped that pile and not another for yards in any direction (although on higher levels there were rocks everywhere), and especially not in that particular scattered cluster.

No, I felt fairly sure that humans had placed most of these rocks here and that if the humans couldn't have been settlers, they had to have been Amerindian people. Once again, though, I had no idea who they were or when they had done so, or why, although I thought tentatively that it was perhaps another burial cairn, except that its placement was so low in the field that this seemed not quite right.

Still, the large burial cairn, now dated well enough to satisfy me, the strange pile of rocks on the floor of the field, the site on the plateau that I privately referred to as the "Blackfoot burial tent" (although it is entirely possible it was placed there, as with the cairn, long before there were a people called Blackfoot, or Siksika, and that it might not have been a burial tent at all), and the vision-quest site (or whatever it was), all merged to mystify, excite, and puzzle me. How was I to find out what had happened here? Especially, how was I to know if I didn't do any digging or disturb any of the rocks or invite archeologists to dig?

What it was I wanted to know I couldn't be precise about. As always, I was far more interested in the spiritual questions I had about the field than I was about facts, such as when the Pelican Lake people had arrived (about thirty-three hundred years ago) or what an Old Wives point looked like, or a Clovis point, or by what name the people might have called themselves. Yet it seemed that I could not answer the former question without some idea about who the various people were who might have traversed the region, and hunted and camped and prayed, and buried some of their dead here, in this beautiful field.

I walked the field, my eyes down, watching out for cactus or half-hopefully for snakes or, without much hope for an elusive point, for flakes and stone tools, for what I didn't know. I thought about the past in this place, what little I knew of it, and I gathered more books and read them, and my feelings grew that archeological data and methods were all too complicated and expert for me to ever make sense of on my own. But still I was convinced that if I had the patience and could maintain my wondering silence well enough and long enough, I would come to understand the field. Something would tell me what I needed to know.

I didn't expect it would be the "voiceless voice" that would explain things to me. Its utterances so far had been as enigmatic as the stone piles themselves, and while after one of them I'd feel as if a light bulb had gone on in my thick brain and new realms of thought had opened for me, any answers were answers I'd come up with myself. And every time I'd heard that voice, it had been so startling, so wonderful, that I'd forgotten to be afraid, and yet never expected I'd hear it again in my life. Nor did I expect I could just say, "Pardon?" or "Would you mind explaining that please?" and get an answer. Dialogue was clearly not a possibility. As to where it had come from, who it was, I had no new ideas, and I still shied away from examining this part of the mystery because I knew that I'd wind up questioning my own sanity.

I began to notice something that hadn't quite come to consciousness before. Not only were there stone circles of varying sizes and with varying configurations of stones on the higher points of the field (and some quite low), I was noticing now that there were also small piles of stones, partly buried in the earth, mostly encrusted with lichen, on nearly every one of the lower hills. Some of these piles still had a few loose stones above the line of the earth, but mostly they consisted of tight clusters of impacted stones just visible above the ground. Puzzling over them, I began to think that they, too, might be—no, must be—burial cairns. Maybe the burial spots of people less illustrious, for whatever reason, than those in the high cairn. As I looked around, I became aware of just how very many of them there were. With this discovery, my certainty of the importance of the field grew.

Many people had been buried here in the field. I didn't, however, see it as a graveyard in quite the sense of the cemetery full of dead people on the high hill outside Eastend. That cemetery had been selected by the townspeople for the purpose probably prior to any deaths, and as people died, for the most part one by one over the years and from different causes, they were buried there in neat rows, side by side, with stone markers to commemorate their lives.

I decided that to make sense of the field, I needed to know about the burial customs of various Plains peoples over the millennia. Many, I read, left their dead on platforms in trees, or made platforms of poles, and returned later, after the flesh was gone, to bundle the bones and bury them. There is archeological evidence that occasionally, rather than waiting, the people stripped away the flesh themselves immediately after a death, bundled the bones, and carried them away with them for later burial elsewhere. Here, of course, there were few trees, and this had been the case beginning about eighty-five hundred years ago when a warm, dry period called the Altithermal occurred (ending about forty-seven hundred years ago) and the boreal forest retreated northward, leaving behind the grasslands of southern Saskatchewan. (This was also when the buffalo as we know them began to appear.) But nearly a mile away from the field, there was a place where a few trees grew naturally, and I speculated that perhaps the bones I felt sure would be under these cairns would once have been on platforms and now would be bundled.

I'd wondered if the stone circle on the plateau was a chief's burial tent, having read that the Siksika would sometimes lay a chief's body in state in his sealed tepee and leave it there. If the grave had been undisturbed, it would be theoretically possible to find the skeletal remains still there in position, possibly under a layer of earth naturally deposited over the years, even though the tepee would long since have weathered away. Perhaps if we dug—which we'd never do—we'd find bones in that stone circle, maybe even the remains of the central peg used to hold down the tepee as had been found at a couple of other sites.

Then I read about mound burials, usually mass graves, and therefore fairly large. Burial mounds have been found on the grasslands, mostly in Manitoba but at least two in southeast Saskatchewan, and so I often looked at small rises in the flat area of the field and wondered if they were man-made, and if so, if there were human remains under them too.

But I felt sure that these many graves, if indeed they were graves, with the exception of the large cairn at the highest point, had been made here because at this particular place many people had died *at the same time.* My growing certainty about this was based only on the similarity of all the small cairns, which were about the same size, with the same size of stones and the same amount and kinds of lichen and moss growing on and around them, and also on a gut feeling for which there was no explanation, except maybe my complete lack of scientific attitude and my childish desire that all of this be the result of some dramatic circumstance.

But if I was correct about this, the people buried here might have died in the historic period during a smallpox epidemic. There are records of a major epidemic which swept the plains between 1780 and 1782. The Snake (or Shoshone) people in the vicinity of the Red Deer River (north and a bit west of here) were dying, and so were the Siksika, who were at that time pushing into the same area. Many Gros Ventre, also hunting on the Canadian Plains, died as well. The Cree, who then lived to the east and the north, are said (by the trader Alexander Henry) to have lost two-thirds of their entire nation. The epidemic so weakened the Shoshone and the Gros Ventre that after the eighteenth century both nations retreated (or were pushed by the Siksika) south into the United States.

Another large epidemic occurred in 1837. The Cree were fortunate in that by this time the traders knew how to vaccinate people and did so, saving many Cree lives. But less fortunate were the Siksika, Nakota, and especially the Mandan of North Dakota, who were reduced by it to a mere twenty-three warriors. (Not long after this the main Mandan village burned to the ground, and the remaining few people dispersed to live with the Hidatsa.) Obviously, it might have been smallpox that had killed the people buried beneath the stone cairns.

But I preferred to think they'd died in battle and that, later, either those who had survived had come back and buried the bodies or others coming upon the dead did so. They had covered each grave or graves with small piles of stones both to protect them from animals and also to inform all other Amerindian people passing by over the ensuing centuries—although I did not know either when this had happened—that this was a sacred site.

That this precise area had been used often and well by ancient peoples was deeply satisfying to me and confirmed what I had, in a vague way, long suspected or thought to be true, but of which I'd never had any proof. Nor had I understood or even thought of the many, highly significant ramifications attendant on this fact, not only for my own life but also for the lives of all the people of Western Canada. My curiosity was aroused about who the dead were and how they lived and when, and that was all.

I paced the field, pausing first at one cairn and then another, and wondered what had happened here. If there'd been a battle here, who were the combatants? Plains Cree and Siksika? As with my unfounded certainty that all these people had died and been buried at the same time (with the exception of the big cairn at the high point), I leaned more and more towards the notion that when it had happened, this had been Siksika territory and, therefore, those buried here were Siksika. I had zero proof of this, although I knew it to be possible, since Siksika territory had once extended from the North Saskatchewan River in Alberta south to the Yellowstone River in Montana, west to the Rocky Mountains and east to 105 degrees of longitude, which is about two-thirds of the way across Saskatchewan.

Cree and Nakota territory was east of that line. They pushed into Siksika territory only in the 1860s as the buffalo began to disappear, and they were forced to go farther west to find them. This invasion of territory had resulted in a lot of deaths in battles all along the boundary, the most famous, and the one that ended the rivalry between Cree and Siksika, occurring in the fall of 1870 at the junction of the Oldman River and St. Mary's River near present-day Lethbridge. The Siksika won decisively, killing between two hundred and three hundred Cree while losing only about forty of their own men. But afterward, rather than allow them to starve, they let the Cree hunt buffalo on their land. So it was also possible that if the deaths occurred in the historic period, the cairns in the field might well be over the remains of Cree or Nakota people.

But there had been other Amerindian peoples here before the Siksika, Cree, and Nakota, who'd been driven out or had moved on south into the United States: the Gros Ventre, the Nez Perce, the Shoshone. I'd found nothing, not points or potsherds or tools, to indicate when whatever had happened here had occurred, which would have been the best clue as to whose graves these were.

I didn't want to call in archeologists. I didn't want them digging up the ground and measuring and disturbing what I now felt certain was a sacred site. I was beginning to feel that our field shouldn't be touched by anyone, at least not anyone not Amerindian. Besides, I had the completely erroneous idea that if I told archeologists offi-cially what I'd found, Peter and I might lose control over the field, so I'd never shown it to anyone in an official capacity.

For years, though, I'd been bringing our guests to the field, some of whom I showed things to, and many more to whom I didn't. My practice of showing so many people had worried me a little and puzzled me, but I was beginning to understand that I did this because I hoped that one of them would be the one who would know, the one who would explain the field to me. One of them, I hoped, would be the *right* person, although so far no one had been. But I hadn't thought this entirely at the conscious level.

My sister came to visit. She brought with her a friend, an Amerindian woman from one of the West Coast peoples, one of the few older people left in her nation who still spoke her own language fluently. As I got to know her a little, I told her about our very inter-esting field. She was eager to see it, and one afternoon the three of us went there to walk through it and study the stone features. I pointed them out, holding nothing back from her. She shared my excitement, recognizing at once that we were in a place that was well out of the ordinary.

I took her up to the vision-quest site. She said she'd like to come back with an offering and pray. Another visitor had given me a braid of sweetgrass, which I gave to her (I am told one must neither sell nor buy sweetgrass, although it happens all the time), and later that day she went by herself and did so, coming back silent and thought-ful, perhaps even troubled.

That evening the sunset was spectacular, and my sister, her friend, and I set out strolling in the warm evening, west down the road. My sister lagged behind, and her friend and I walked ahead, talking about the field. She was so moved by what she'd seen there that suddenly she left me and went off the road and into a high spot in the grass, where she faced the field, raised her arms as I'd once "seen" a shaman do, and called out to the field in her own language. I stood behind her, watching her, not sure what was happening.

A voice answered from deep in the heart of the hills, a strange, weird cry such as I'd never heard before. (My sister said later, "I thought it was a woman.") I took it for coyotes, although I'd never heard one sound like that. Shivers ran down my back, I turned away to leave the friend so as to give her privacy—I thought the spirits were answering her. But in great excitement she called to me to come to her side.

"Look!" she said. "Do you see them?" We stared into the shadowed hills. I saw nothing out of the ordinary. "The people," she said. "They're moving around, fast. Don't you see them?" But no matter how I stared, concentrating, I saw only the darkening flanks of the hills, the sharp line where they met the sky.

In time, she came back to the road, my sister caught up with us, and as night fell, we went back to the house. She said only that she had a bad feeling about the field, that she felt sure that something bad had happened there.

Soon they'd returned to the West Coast, and a few weeks later, I received a phone call from my sister in which she told me that not long after she and her friend had reached home, her friend had been walking in the mall in a nearby community when a very old Amerindian man, his hair in braids, someone she did not know at all, simply veered out of the crowd and came up to her as if he knew her. He said, "I have to get back to Saskatchewan. I have to look after my ancestors." He told her that he came from a reserve in Saskatchewan near the Montana border. Many of his ancestors had been killed in skirmishes with the army, and no ceremonies had ever been performed for them to put them to rest. Our friend replied, "Don't worry, old man. I'll take care of it for you."

I felt that I knew at last what had happened in the field.

But time passed, and even this, which I accepted wholly as a perfectly fitting way of receiving the necessary revelation about so mysterious a place, ceased to satisfy. It began instead to increase my desire to know which people, what date, the facts of the matter.

It seemed to me, finally, that the best course would be to find elders and speak with them, but one does not simply knock on the door of an elder, request information, and expect to get it. I didn't think that in that direction I had a hope, unless I got luckier than I had any reason to think I might be, unless it was all foreordained and any day now an elder with the stories of that time were to knock on my door. This I knew to be more than merely absurd; it was beyond absurd.

For weeks I was stymied in my writing and thinking as I pondered this question, wondering how to approach an elder, and what elder, where? I thought maybe in Montana there might be old people who would know the story, but I knew no one in Montana, especially not any Amerindian people, and I didn't have the courage to approach anyone on the reservations there. But I did feel that it was imperative for this book that somehow I find out, in historical terms, the details about the people whose graves I so often walked among.

One foggy, nasty day as I was driving home, on a sudden impulse I stopped my car, got out, crossed a pasture, climbed a fence, and walked into the field. I climbed a low hill and stood staring up at the higher hills, first in one direction and then another. The fog was thick but constantly moving and changing, allowing me glimpses of first this patch of hills and then that one. I stared hard, as if when the fog broke apart, the answer would be written there on the grassy slopes.

In the distance to the east, the west, and the south, the fog began to dissipate, but the stretch of hills where I stood was still partially shrouded in a moving cloud of mist. As I watched, the last shreds of mist moved away from them so that they were fully visible.

I looked up at the clean, bright flanks, dotted with stones and full of the burrows of animals and the home of the giant snake, and over which a people I did not know and could not see had once walked. I waited, thinking of the day my sister's friend had called out in her own language across the long sweeps of grass to where these hills rose towards the sky. Now I called out into the silence and the stillness, *What happened here?*

There was no sound in reply, but as I watched, suddenly a thick blanket of fog swept in again and covered the hills, until I couldn't see them at all, even while all around me, to the east, west, and to the south, even the low hill on which I stood, there was sunshine. Only the hills to which I had directed my question were obscured. It was as if the spirits of the field had answered my question, and the answer was, *You will never know.*

Now I walked among the silent stones with new puzzlement and new yearning. The field seemed to me as full of presence as any occupied house and more so than any church ever had. I had heard voices here, although they'd been only in my head, not outside me, and had been soundless in any case, just words that seemed to be from some other soul not my own, from a presence formless and unseen and unidentified. Except that I had "seen" a shaman there, and I'd once caught a glimpse of a cluster of Amerindian women.

I felt there was great wisdom in the field, it gleamed from the grassy, rock-strewn slopes and in the coming and going of cloudy shadows and patches of brightness, it was carried on the wind and rippled the grasses, it hovered all about me on the very air. What was it? Where did it come from?

One day I suddenly realized that I was probably wrong in attributing to Nature itself—herself—all the strange experiences I'd had out on the prairie since I'd arrived here, having no better idea of their source and paying far too much attention to what others had written and said. I thought of the haunting of our house.

Now I wondered if this disembodied presence or presences that I felt so strongly, that answered questions for me, that gave me help and advice, that probed my psyche sometimes as I waited humbly, head bowed, helpless and gratefully so, to whatever haunted the vast space between me and the earth and the distant blue of the sky, was not God (whatever that might be) or even Nature (whatever that might be), but the restless spirits of the many unhonoured dead of this field.

Chapter 8

THE MOON

PETER AND I HAD BEEN IN A DISTANT CITY TO ATTEND A dinner. It was March and there had been flooding all over the West, in Canada and the United States. Eastend, set in a once-in-a-hundred-year flood plain, was not exempt from this, and the Frenchman River was so high that the town authorities were considering whether it should be evacuated or not, as had happened once before in 1952. As we approached home, we could see that the road to our place was in low spots completely underwater, and judging by the fact that the fenceposts on each side of the road at the lowest spot had vanished, we knew the water was too deep for even a tractor to go through. Peter pulled to the side of the road, took out the cellphone, and began to dial a friend in town to find out if the roads leading there were underwater too, since it seemed to him that our only recourse was to find a bed overnight in town.

I did not want to stay in town overnight, although why it seemed to me absolutely unbearable to do so is, in retrospect, very strange. I knew it would inconvenience whomever we stayed with, but I also knew that we would never be turned away, might even be welcomed; but no matter what, I simply could not contemplate taking this measure.

Let me preface this story by saying that I am famous among my friends for my great common sense, for my ability to examine the contingencies before I act, and that no one who knows me well ever says of me that I might be expected to take crazy chances. And I am absolutely not daring in a physical sense, as a result, I like to tell myself, of my small size and lack of physical strength and of my upbringing in which our mother definitely discouraged adventurousness.

But now, to my own surprise, I said, "Peter, I'm walking in." I reminded him that since we were expected back tonight, no one was feeding our dog and cats; in fact, no one had been able to get in to do it while we were away, although this had been only since the previous morning. He was still talking on the phone and, I think, only half heard me. I was using the dog and cats as an excuse to do what I knew I would do anyway, over what I was sure would be his objections, as he is always more laid-back than I am, takes much longer to make up his mind about courses of action, and worries considerably less than I do about just about everything.

I said again, "I'm walking in!" He put the phone down for a moment and pointed out that since he'd just had knee surgery for arthritis, he didn't feel physically able to walk that two miles over the uneven, hilly ground. Undeterred, I told him, "You drive into town then, and phone me when you get there. I'll be at home by then." There was only about a half-hour left before darkness, and I was desperate to get through the hills and onto the built-up road before nightfall. Instead of answering me, he dialled another number.

"I'm going now!" I said, and opened the door. I think I was both waiting for and wanting him to say, "Please don't go, it isn't safe," and trying desperately to leave before he did, because I knew it would stop me. Translation: I was afraid, both of going and of not going.

He began to speak to someone on the phone again, and I leaped out of the vehicle, shut the door behind me, and set out up the nearby draw as fast as I could, hurrying towards home in the gathering darkness. I was as one possessed, I see now, and even then, in the back of my mind, I think I knew I was. I didn't contemplate the unreasonableness of my actions, though. We might not be 100 per cent welcome in the households where we might have stayed, but any irritation our hosts might have with the situation would be well hidden, since the first imperative in any pioneering community is still to give hospitality to anyone in need, even to one's worst enemy. I could not explain my fervid determination to get home, and I didn't try. I was going, that was all.

I was wearing my city clothes: pantyhose and slip, long, flared denim skirt, shin-high winter boots, and a lightweight down-filled jacket over a blouse and sweater. I was wearing lined leather gloves, but no scarf on my head. It was March, after all, the temperature was hovering just around freezing, but it was windless, and I felt warmly enough dressed, and the moon was full, or nearly full, so the light for the last section of my trip, which would be after nightfall, would be bright enough to see my way.

Luckily, the area I had to cross to get to the road leading home was a patch of hills (including the field) that I knew, if not intimately, at least pretty well. The area was too big for me to fix all of it firmly in my memory: the location of each rock, each large badger hole, stretch of hardpan, and patch of cactus. But I knew where the Amerindian graves were, or at least where the piles of rocks, the cairns, the stone circles were, and the man-made trail, and the fences, and farther on, some drainage ditches. I was counting on my knowledge, plus luck—not breaking my leg in a badger hole or falling into a prickly pear cactus—to get me home safely.

In the growing twilight I headed first through the draws of a neighbour's land, past stone circles and large rocks with shaved sides where a hundred or a thousand years earlier, I knew, Amerindian people had broken off large pieces to use in tool-making. I set my mental compass for the lowest corner on our land, closest to the flat stretch that led down to the road which I would follow home. The moon was rising now, and although it was growing darker, I still could see my way fairly well.

I knew perfectly well the sensible route was to walk the top of the hills home instead of skirting them and following the lowest fields, but I wanted to avoid at all cost walking through the field and my route was planned to avoid it entirely. I knew the field to be full of ghosts, and I knew, too, that the spirit world is not always benign. I would never willingly choose to walk through that area by myself after dark.

Coyotes were singing to the west across the fields as I set out, and I didn't want to meet a pack of coyotes either out there in the darkness. I had a third misgiving. Range cattle were grazing in all the fields I had to cross, and I was approaching each rise cautiously, peering ahead in the failing light and staying as close as possible to a fence I could duck under if I startled them and they charged, or even just crowded around me. And yet I went alone, I headed out into the night when I did not have to, when no one was trying to persuade me to go, when the reasons I had for going made little sense—weren't actually reasons at all.

Now I was through the first patch of hills and draws and had arrived at the fence corner I'd been aiming for. I saw spread out before me the wide flat piece of land that stretched out to meet the road. It was completely flooded, underwater, with snow and ice-covered hillocks rising up a few inches here and there across the plain, which in drier times wasn't quite a plain, but a bumpy, gopher-and-badger-holed, greasewood, cactus-and-sagebrush-dotted field that at the extremity where I was standing was traversed by a deep, narrow drainage ditch before rising up into hills, and at the far edge, before the road, dropped into a deep, two-metre-wide ditch. In between the two borders, I knew somewhere out there, although I wasn't sure exactly where, there was another drainage ditch wider than either of the other two, but not quite as deep. It had completely vanished under the moonlight-bright sheet of ice-and-snow-dotted water. I knew that our cattle were out there somewhere on the road or on the higher land, but I couldn't see or hear them.

I hesitated for a brief moment, but the irrational drive to get home had not lessened and, if anything, had intensified. I set out, heading east along the fenceline, above the flooded field. At that point, if I could have gone straight south, I would have reached our yard by a direct path to it, but now I was heading east, looking for a place to cross the water-filled ditch. A few yards along, I came to an icy snowbank that stretched downward across the ditch, filling it, which would provide me with passage into the field. I half walked, half crawled down it, sinking in to my thighs where it was more icy slush than solid snow.

My boots were only mid-calf height and had long since been filled with ice and snow, and my legs, clad only in sheer pantyhose, had grown very cold. My long denim skirt was soaked above my knees, but—until I made a misstep and fell on one side and got soaked up to my shoulder—my jacket was still dry. Since all of this was taking much longer than I'd expected, night had fallen, but I kept thanking my lucky stars because the moon, so large and white in the sky, radiated a cold but clear, strong light, which made it possible for me to see, at least for a short distance around me, almost as well as in daylight.

I righted myself after my fall and balanced on a tiny hillock looking out across the quarter-mile or so of icy water through which I would have to wade to reach the safety of the road. I thought: It is such a little way, and I am already wet almost to my waist, and my boots are already full of cold water. If I cross it, I can make it to my house in minutes. At the same time another part of my mind was telling me: It is madness to plunge into that freezing water, especially when you are already wet and very cold. And how will you cross that ditch that you know is out there somewhere in that field? Don't do it! Go back!

I hesitated maybe ten seconds, if that, and struck out wading. The water rose up above my knees to my thighs, but I kept going, stumbling, half-falling, but saving myself, splashing the water up my jacket. My gloves were soaked; I was completely soaked from my shoulder down on one side and on the other had a huge wet patch on my chest. As the water deepened, I got wet to my chest. The moon had risen higher now and hung full and perfect and white in the sky over my left shoulder. In its light I could see everything I needed to see.

I stopped suddenly, alarmed by the splashing of water in the distance. The noise I was making had alarmed the cattle, which were far over on the eastern edge of the field but lost in darkness so that I couldn't see them. They were panicked, galloping through deep water, although I couldn't see them and could only guess which way they were running. I paused, scared to death. I knew they'd run right over me and not even notice in their fright. After a moment the sound of their rushed passage through water stopped, and I knew they'd reached the road, which was still above water. I prayed they would settle there and not come to the section of road where I hoped in moments to emerge. I kept going.

Suddenly I paused. Somehow I knew that I had found the submerged ditch, that I was right at its edge. Probably the clue was some change in the temperature and depth of the water, but I knew I was there, and once again I stopped, trying to decide whether to plunge ahead or turn back. I told myself in rising alarm and amazement at my own craziness, Don't! Go back! But the strange, driven self said, "You're already soaked, so what if you get a little wetter? You'll be home in a few minutes." As if lives depended on my getting home. I knew I was risking my health, maybe even my life, by going on, but I didn't seem to care. I hesitated, folded my long jacket up around my waist, and plunged into the water-filled ditch.

I had not gone two steps before I realized I was in trouble. The bottom foot or two of the ditch was an icy gumbo of snow and mud, and I was sinking into it. I wasn't sure I could get out. I saw that the only way to cross the ditch was to throw myself forward and swim, and I actually contemplated doing so. But I was wearing heavy winter boots, a bulky, long winter jacket, a long, heavy denim skirt—I wasn't sure I could swim in them even the five or six feet to the far bank. Nor was I sure now that I could get out of the half-frozen mush I was standing in, having sunk by this time to halfway up my shins. For the first time I had an instant's real, concrete fear that bordered on terror. Behind it, though, was this same famous common sense asking myself if I had completely taken leave of my senses to have gotten myself into such a terrifying mess for absolutely no reason.

In retrospect, I think this was the moment when my madness,

whatever had driven me into this situation, left me, and if not sanity, at least the instinct for self-preservation took the upper hand. I kicked hard to free myself from the mud, floated upwards, managed a partial turn suspended in the freezing water, and kicking and stretching out with my arms, made it back to the relative safety of the plain I had just crossed. I saw then that I no longer had any choice but to go back the way I'd come, to walk to a neighbour's house and phone Peter, who, I was sure, would by now be safely ensconced in a friend's warm house in town.

I couldn't feel my legs anymore. I surveyed the water-logged field I'd just crossed and looked up into the darkened hills. I didn't know how much time had passed since I'd started this trip, but guessed it to be about an hour, and I knew I had to get to warmth very soon. Looking up into the night, I couldn't tell which way I'd come, what my route had been, and I wasn't sure now that I could still lift my legs. I think if at this point I had faltered, I might very well have died out there, a mile from home, a mile from a neighbour's. I would have died from hypothermia and/or perhaps by drowning when I couldn't save myself any longer.

I knew without thinking about it that I had to find a place to stand that was up out of the freezing water, even if only for a moment. There was nowhere that I could see, except for, here and there, greasewood bushes rising above the water. I stepped up and began to stand on them, and as they crackled and crunched under my feet and began to sink, I'd head for the next one. So between a few steps of wading in thigh-deep ice water, I'd give myself and my numb legs a moment's respite as I balanced on the frozen bushes. By this time I was clear-headed, thinking only of how to get back to safety, looking ahead in the bright moonlight for the safest, quickest route; I often couldn't tell what might work and what wouldn't, so sometimes, misjudging the distance between clumps of grease-wood or the depth of water, I'd fall, then have to backtrack and try a different route.

It was cold, it was dark in the distance, although on the right and around me the moon shone very brightly on the water and the snow. Off to my left on the line of the hills, I saw a number of red lights, like the taillights of trucks idling with their headlights turned off, and they seemed to be sitting up there, the occupants of the trucks watching my progress towards safety. I smiled to myself, thinking, if that isn't just like Peter. When he phoned the house and I wasn't there, he became alarmed and organized a search party for me. Ahead of me also, glimpsed through the draws as I climbed and moved back to my starting point on the grid road, I could see more red lights, and I was sure that one of them was our vehicle with Peter in it, directing things. I kept going, encouraged, moving as fast as I could towards warmth. This time I went straight through the field I'd been avoiding, never mind ghosts, never mind coyotes; in the face of a more immediate danger my fear of both of them diminished and almost disappeared.

Finally I reached the last quarter-mile before safety, and striding rapidly through a low spot between hills, I was out of sight of all the red taillights of various vehicles, nor could I see them. Once again I was alone with the snow and the rocks and the moonlight-bright darkness. I began to feel—and this is not easy to describe—a kind of warmth, as one feels when someone loving is near, like a child bask-ing in the warmth of its mother's love, or much-loved wife held in the arms of her husband. I looked up and to the right and knew it was coming from the moon.

I did not really question this. The sensation was far too strong; it was unquestionable, absolute. The moon's visage was a pale gold, and she was as large as I've ever seen her as she shone her warm beams of love down on me from her place low in the sky above the silent, spirit-ridden, indigo hills. I felt completely safe and cared for as, smiling to myself, I hurried on through the last hills to where I knew Peter sat in our truck waiting for me to arrive.

At last I came to the place where a couple of hours earlier we'd parked. Our vehicle was just where it had been when I jumped out of it, but Peter was not in it, it was cold and dark, and where the vehicle was was not where I'd seen the red taillights. There were no taillights anywhere, no vehicles at all on the road or on the high line of the hills to the west where I'd reassured myself when, all alone and afraid, I hurried back towards safety.

I was alone, half-frozen, bewildered, and unable to understand why our truck was there but Peter wasn't in it. Still labouring under the effects of all this madness, I could not make sense of what had happened. But the vehicle was unlocked, so I got in, used my own keys to turn on the motor and the heater on high, searched in my bag for dry clothes, with some difficulty peeled off my frozen, wet ones, and struggled into dry ones. Then I used the cellphone to call town, where Peter hadn't arrived and no one knew where he was. Nor was he at the neighbour's or anywhere else I thought he might be. I couldn't think what to do.

By this time I was warm and rested, and I wondered if I should maybe start out again for home, this time taking the sensible high route. But I thought of all those cattle I'd heard running through the deep water, and I didn't know where they were and wasn't sure I'd be able to find a safe route past them. And where was Peter? What had happened to all those trucks I thought were full of people searching for me? Plainly, I must have been wrong about all that. But I'd seen them! And what about the moon, still shining up there in the sky, but so distant now, grown smaller, no longer paying any attention to me.

Then I saw through a break in the hills from the direction I'd just come, a pair of headlights coming overland. I turned our truck so that it was facing in that direction and flashed the headlights off and on. The headlights kept appearing and disappearing as whatever vehicle it was manoeuvred its way up and down the hills and around obstacles. When it came nearer, I jumped out of the truck and ran towards the lights, and then it arrived and it was Peter, driving our all-terrain vehicle.

In fact, there had been no search party, no red lights on the hills or on the road except the ones that were always there. After I'd left the truck, Peter had decided perhaps if he took his cane, and his time, and took the high route, he could walk home after all. He did so with no trouble, even remarked on what a pleasant walk it had been in the balmy air and the moonlight, and when he reached the house and saw I wasn't there, he'd changed his clothes, checked the messages on the answering machine, gathered up a blanket to wrap me in and a warm scarf and heavy winter mitts, gone to the Quonset, started the four-wheeler, and headed out to find me. When he told me this, puzzled by me as he often is, but assured and calm in his steady role as rescuer, handing me the scarf and mitts and wrapping the blanket around my legs as I climbed onto the four-wheeler behind him, I didn't know whether to laugh or cry or check myself into the nearest psychiatric facility. I did a little of the first two but have so far managed to evade the third.

So much about that night baffles and amazes me, but what made me laugh in the most rueful fashion was the picture of Peter strolling along in the moonlight, enjoying himself up there as he crossed the tops of the hills, while at the same time, far below on the flat land, I was struggling and terrified and fighting for my very life. It seemed, and seems, to me more than merely a fact of the occasion, but also a metaphor for our two different approaches to life, our two different passages through the world: Peter so purely physical, so in tune with his ranching world and with the prairie he'd spent his life on, so solid and stable in every way; me, tense, fearful, a good deal more concerned with the progress of my soul than with my body, questioning everything and then questioning the answers.

And what was that about the moon? I don't think I told Peter, or anyone else, that part. But that same spring I did a small book tour through eight cities in the American West arranged by my American publisher, Hungry Mind Press. In Missoula, Montana, I told this story to an audience, for the most part as bemused by it as I was myself.

But when it was over, a woman in the audience came up to me and said, "Do you know the story of the boys who ran with the antelope?" I said that I didn't. She said, briefly, that they had been enchanted and had run with them until they had died.

"Our people," she said—here I could only guess that she must be Amerindian, although I would not have known this by her appearance; but I did observe something unusual about her way of speaking which I couldn't quite put my finger on—"have a story about following the moon to your death ..." or perhaps it was "the moon calling you to your death." She ended by saying, gazing at me in a very serious, careful, and, I thought, assessing way, "Be careful of the moon!"

An Amerindian living in Missoula, Montana, might belong to any of many nations, and I had no way of knowing which one. I have searched through my books about Amerindian life, beliefs, rituals, but I have not paid much attention to books of their stories, and in any case, my collection is not at all comprehensive. I do know, though, that the moon is enspirited and is a powerful person in the world of many Plains Amerindian people. And a Haisla friend had said to me that she had been told that red lights are spirits. At the time, she was speaking in a different context and was trying to recover her childhood teaching about what we would call witchcraft, or sorcery. (In my reading of stories about the "shaking tent," when those present see lights, they are helping spirits and they are blue and green.) The implication was that red lights would be dangerous and/or misleading, although in this case, even if they were completely misleading, the delusion they caused me to labour under was a comforting one.

I puzzled and puzzled over what had happened that night, particularly that very powerful feeling I had of the moon personified, gazing down at me and flooding me with beams of love so that I lost all my fear and felt as a much-loved child again. Clearly, it was all an enchantment. And then I wondered what the purpose of it might be. Was it a test? A test of what? Of my courage? My inner strength? And the warmth I felt from that huge, pale-gold moon was a sign of having passed the test? A test that would lead to what? For what journey or gift or task? I confess that all the heroic quests of mythology went through my mind, and the gifts the successful heroes received for their valour. None of it made any sense to me in the context of my own ordinary life. It was all just another mystery I had to live with, I thought, and in the hope that one day what it was all about would come clear to me.

But after that I would look up at the moon in the sky in all her phases and wonder how she could be both a goddess having control over life and death and, at the same time, a lightless, cold, dead rock hurtling through space, for I was beginning to suspect, even though

I could not see how or find an explanation that satisfied me, that she was indeed both.

Robin Ridington, in a paper called "Monsters and the Anthropologist's Reality," says of the Dunne-za, a people of the Peace River region of British Columbia:

> The Dunne-za represented the sun and moon as a person, not because they misunderstood their physical nature, but because they recognized in the systematic relationships of celestial motion a metaphor for transformations of human phenomenology. In order to understand their metaphor we must translate between their phenomenology and ours, not simply between two conceptions of astronomical reality. Their knowledge of celestial mechanics was accurate and pragmatic rather than fanciful and uninformed.

I agree with his interpretation, but after my experiences in the field, especially of my baffling and frightening struggle through ice, snow, and water under the watchful moon, I would omit the word "metaphor."

Chapter 9

THE SPIRIT OF THE LAND

ALMOST THIRTY YEARS AGO NOW, WHEN I WAS TEACHING a class of teenagers with learning difficulties in the Saskatoon school system, I attended a teachers' conference. Although I had no Amerindian children in my classes and there were at the time perhaps only two in the entire inner-city school where I worked, I chose to attend a session given by two Amerindian male lecturers on, I thought, the needs of Amerindian children in the classroom. There were only perhaps fifteen to twenty people in the audience, all women, I think, and all elementary school teachers. I recall the two leaders of the session each speaking quietly for a while and showing some slides, although I can't remember of what. I think they called for questions. Hands went up.

A woman in her late thirties or early forties and nicely dressed spoke first. She asked what we might do, specifically what *she* might do, to help these children. The two male lecturers glanced briefly at each other, their faces revealing nothing at all—I remember thinking that this was deliberate, that they were hiding emotion— and then simply went on talking, ignoring her question. It was as if she hadn't spoken at all. She didn't ask another question, I'm not sure that anyone else did either, and the session ended very soon after that.

For nearly thirty years I pondered that incident, trying to understand it, and mostly failing. Why would you ignore such a question, I asked myself? Because it was a stupid question? Because it was unanswerable without a basis of understanding or information that plainly wasn't there, so that the lecturers found it most polite to simply pretend it hadn't happened? And what was it that the woman who asked the question—and me, too, and everybody else in the audience—failed to know? Or was it simply (as I'm sure I thought at the time) that they were men and we were women and they had no respect for us to start with? But although I was and continue to be always on the alert for such built-in contempt of the feminine, I did not really think it was operative in that instance.

I think I see now the built-in racism in the well-intentioned question, the implication that Amerindian children needed something different, something more. And perhaps that is all that the two lecturers were reacting to. But it seemed to me there was more than that to it, although I was never able to be clear about what it was, beyond thinking that the question itself indicated a failure to see the world in any terms but those of a middle-class person whose cultural roots were in Europe.

A year or two ago I was working in my kitchen and had the radio tuned to our beloved CBC. A tape was being played of an incident at a teachers' conference, once again in Saskatoon, and an Amerindian woman was on the stage. Apparently the lecture she'd given had just ended, and the floor was open for questions. The sound of the question coming from the floor, a woman again, was muffled and distant but clear enough that I knew she was asking the same question the woman had asked in the session I'd attended thirty years earlier. "What can I do to help Amerindian children in my classroom?" The speaker shot back, her voice cracking with anger, "*You can admit that you're the problem!*" In an instant she got a grip on herself and added some qualifying remark that marginally took the sting out of her accusation, but I doubt very much that anybody in that audience, which sounded as if it were large, was much fooled by it. She was very angry, again I thought, at what she saw as the unconscious racism in the question, so angry that for an instant she couldn't hide it.

Standing in my kitchen more than two hundred miles away, I was more or less stunned by her open rage, especially coming from an Amerindian woman, something I'd never heard before, by the sudden memory of the almost identical incident, and by the fact that they had occurred thirty years apart. Plainly, I wasn't going to be able to forget this; I was going to have to give it a lot of thought, because I knew it meant something important, that some-how all of this was material for a book I hoped to write, once I could figure out what it was about and how to write it. My hands were wet with dishwater, but I wiped them fast on my jeans and grabbed a pencil and made an illegible note on a pad by the phone of the speaker's name and the date and what she had said. Then time passed and I lost the note.

If the school system in Saskatchewan, the public schools in the cities now full of Amerindian children, and also the large Amerindian community in our cities have changed a great deal in the intervening thirty years between the two incidents, it was plain, too, that the sensibilities and even the information base of the rest of us in Saskatchewan hadn't changed nearly enough. Now I knew this, as I hadn't thirty years earlier; I was even beginning at last to realize—aside from the unconscious racist basis of the two questions of which I was also guilty—what else was missing from the under-standing of the two questioners.

I was beginning to comprehend this, finally, through my more than twenty years here, as I like to say, living in the landscape. For the most part I was being taught it by the landscape, by Nature itself, and specifically by my experiences in the field. But sadly I was not learning it from long conversations with Amerindian people. As I've said, there are virtually no Amerindian people in southwest Saskatchewan except for the one reserve north of here. They were driven out in the 1880s by the starvation policy of Lieutenant-Governor Dewdney (1881–1888) after the buffalo were gone and many of the leaders refused to "take treaty" because they under-stood all too well what this would mean to their people. (I am told that the Nakota people, now of Carry the Kettle Reserve, were force-marched three hundred miles east of here to their reserve, although the "force-marched" interpretation depends on whom one is talking to—Amerindian or non-Amerindian.) It is also instructive to learn that leaders of the Blackfoot nation, plus the Plains Cree and Lakota people, wished to have all of southwest Saskatchewan for contiguous reserves, making an Indian homeland, a situation the people in power couldn't contemplate since they saw the massing of Amerindian people as far too dangerous.

I'd been given a few hints of understanding from books. My first clue was the day that I realized that those eloquent and moving speeches of the old leaders, now the ancestors, were not metaphoric at all, as all we Europeans chose to understand them, but actual. Though we saw such speeches as childish and faintly silly, if also eloquent, I knew now that *they meant every word they said*. We just could not comprehend this.

Over and over again I've thought back to my childhood in a

village on the banks of the Saskatchewan River where the many Amerindian and Métis children were often shunned and taunted by non-native children. I had been taught that *if they were inferior to us* (this part was unspoken) we must nonetheless never show it in any way and must never verbally abuse anyone who was different from us, no matter who, but especially not the dark-skinned children in our village. If our parents had taught us that we must never say such things, they didn't say we couldn't think them, and the society around us had no such compunctions.

I have carried around with me since I was six years old the shame of something that happened one hot summer day when we girls had been playing in two separate groups. We had become angry with each other and quarrelled as children do, and I broke the rule I'd been raised with. I said to another little girl, "Why is your skin so dark!" as an accusation, as the final, clinching line of our conflict. I was saying, in fact: You're only an Indian, and I am not, so of course you lose. How I have since despised myself for that and wished to find some way to make up for it.

Since that incident as a six-year-old, which I've carried around with me like a stone in my heart, I've had very few dealings with Amerindian people. I was a student in the days when Amerindian children went to residential, not public, schools, and I was a school-teacher in the days before a significant number of Amerindian people had moved into the cities to live, sending their children to the public schools. When I taught at the university, the few Amerindian professors taught in their own departments of Native Studies or Indian Education with nearly all Amerindian students, and our paths never crossed. It wasn't until I came to southwest Saskatchewan to live, into the one area of the province where nearly all Amerindian people had been driven out a century earlier, that I began to think about them, that I found I could not forget them, that I began to study what I could find about them and their history, that I began at last, although still very rarely, to meet them.

My interest grew, my desire to know more kept expanding and nagging at me. I would probably not have been able to say, when this first began to happen, why it was, but thinking back, I see that my insatiable desire *to know* about them grew out of the experiences I was beginning to have on the land, out of the land, from the land. I wanted to know what all the stone circles were for, what they meant, and how the people who created them might have under-stood the land I was so slowly and so minimally coming to know: the plants, the animals, the seasonal variations of both. How did it *look* to them? What did it *mean* to them? What did they know? How did they know it? How did they understand Spirit? How did they know about Spirit? And on and on.

I slowly came to know that much that was being published by people with cultural roots primarily in Europe about Amerindian belief systems was false, that there was much charlatanism out there in response to our rising interest in Amerindian ways and beliefs. Also, that much of it was dangerous and sometimes despicable in its theft of what was left to a conquered people. I wanted to peel all of that back to find the truths. I had only two resources to help me do this: books and the land itself.

When my husband and I finally concluded the arrangements to turn the Butala ranch into the Old Man On His Back Prairie and Heritage Preserve, an evening celebration was to be held in the local community hall. The people of the nearby reserve were invited to stage their own celebration during the day as a blessing on the new preserve. They chose a site and planned to build a sweat lodge and hold a sweat bath and to follow this with a feast and a round dance. Because it was our doing and our land, they invited Peter and me to take part in their ceremonies, especially to join the sweat-bath ceremony.

About this last I had strong misgivings. I have suffered from vary-ing degrees of claustrophobia since my labour when my son was born, and in the last ten or so years I have developed a pretty severe asthma-like reaction to cigarette smoke if I inhale it directly, and I am generally very sensitive now to air that isn't fresh. As well as these physical conditions, I've had enough experiences of the supernat-ural, as this book will testify, to be afraid of them. But I changed in the back of somebody's van into a pair of shorts and a sleeveless low blouse, and when people began to move into the sweat lodge and beckoned to me, I went, trying not to show how scared I was.

Nor did I know anything practical about this ritual. I didn't know that once you go into the lodge and seal it up, you don't stay there forever, that there is in fact a set sequence of songs and prayers to be gone through in each of (at least, in this case) four separate sessions, each of which lasts perhaps twenty minutes to half an hour. In between each sequence the passage is opened and everyone goes outside and gets fresh air and rests before the sweat goes on. No one had in any way prepared me for this by even telling me this simple fact. As I was walking in, the woman enter-ing beside me told me I needed a towel and a blanket, and I had to go back and get them.

We women sat on one side and the men on the other. I watched the people filing in, was surprised at how very many there were, and saw to my growing horror that a number of the men were carrying lit cigarettes that they hadn't finished smoking. More and more people came in and sat down, and I began to worry that there would be no fresh air to breathe at all, worse, that it would be full of cigarette smoke and I would have an asthma attack and choke and die on the spot. I was so scared that I almost jumped up and ran out as the keeper of the door began to replace the canvas and hides to seal us in. Something held me back, and it wasn't common sense, but a kind of clumsy attempt at courtesy.

When the heat began to rise and I felt I couldn't breathe, I was close to panic, but an older woman seated beside me whispered in my ear to lie down and put my face in the grass and it would be easier to breathe when it got really hot. I reached behind and tried to squeeze my fingers between the earth and the canvas and blankets covering the willow frame. I thought if I could even feel the air outside, I'd be able to stand the heat and lack of oxygen—a part of me knew my real problem was simple fear—but the coverings were stretched so tightly that I couldn't push my fingers between them and the earth.

I was too afraid to stop fighting the physical occasion, the steam, the sensation I had of not being able to breathe. I couldn't bring myself simply to go with what was happening, not wanting to lose myself in the experience for fear of what might happen. I *knew* what might happen: spirits, voices, visions. I suppose I was really afraid of losing control. So I held on and squirmed and threw myself around in a panic, and the kind, good woman next to me whispered, "Do you want to go out?" And I thought, You mean I can go out if I want to? I'd thought I was stuck there until I died or went insane. "Yes," I said. "Please!"

She hesitated for a minute, but then she called out in Cree, and voices went around the men's side in Cree, calling to each other, and the shaking of rattles or leafy branches or whatever it was died away, and the singing; and then people called to the man seated outside the entrance, and he called back, then began to open the canvas, and finally I could escape and I did. The voices behind me started up again with their chanting, and then I realized I had done something shameful.

I walked away, so upset by what I had done that I couldn't really grasp it, couldn't really understand it, just had this sensation of some appalling cloud hovering around me that would soon descend and crush me. That there would be no escape from it, that I had done this myself. I went across the field, past the mothers rocking babies, and other women who hadn't gone in and were waiting for the sweat to end, and down into a deep coulee behind them. I kept walking. I was gone perhaps a half-hour, the whole time the realization of what I'd done growing bigger and bigger, not gaining in clarity, no mitigating circumstances appearing to me, and when I finally started back to the camp, I met one of the women coming to look for me.

I said to her that I had just realized that I was going to have to live with what I'd done for the rest of my life. She must have replied, but I can't remember anything she said. I remember also that I said to her that maybe after all, instead of there being anything special about me with regard to her people, I was just another one of those people fascinated by Indian people and their beliefs. She said little, but the fact she'd come looking for me and walked back with me, never saying a word of chastisement or showing the slightest anger or even disdain, was the only comfort I've been able to take from the whole episode. (In fact, later she asked me if I'd be interested in being a volunteer at Okimaw Ohci Healing Lodge on the Nekaneet reserve, an institution for federally sentenced aboriginal women run on native spirituality principles.)

When I got back to the camp, everybody had left the sweat and was recovering in preparation for the next round. Seeing this, I said to the elder who'd invited us that if I'd known it would be over in a few minutes, I would have been able to stick it out to the end. I said that I had known for days I was going to have to do this, and I'd been afraid, but felt that I had to. The elder watched me closely, then asked me, "Do you want to go again?" All the people around us were rising now and re-entering the lodge. I hesitated for an instant, but then I said, "No!" shaking my head vigorously. Even as I said this, I knew I was wrong, but I did it anyway. I thought that perhaps some day I'd be able to, but never then. I no longer know, if I ever did, what it was I was resisting at that moment, and it has even crossed my mind to wonder if my refusal was merely self-punishment for the way I'd shamed myself and damaged the ceremony for others.

At the celebratory supper that night in the hall I tried to go around to every table where the people of the reserve sat—thinking back, I don't believe there was any mixing of locals with the Amerindian people—and say to them who I was and that I was glad they had come. At a table of men I tried to explain why I had run out of the sweat lodge, and they laughed, and one of them caught my hand and teased me, but one of them turned his body away from me, his face set, wouldn't look at me or speak to me, and I was ashamed and remorseful and wanted to explain to him and ask him to forgive me.

That shaming episode taught me something else. Fascinated by and admiring of it as I am, I find I don't really want to *live* in the traditional Plains Amerindian world as some non-aboriginal people I've met or read about have done, giving up everything they'd been raised in, from material goods to Christianity and their own culture's value system. Despite being very critical of it, I'm not completely alienated from the world I was raised in. I think, also, that it's too late for that.

I'm a hybrid. I've been taught European culture as the only kind of culture that counts, and I've cherished it and wished very much, to have more of it than my birthplace and position in life will allow me. Of all things in life I love books best, and writing, and then the other arts, especially painting. But because I'm third-generation Canadian and westerner on one side and, on the other, Canadian since 1650 and westerner since 1911, and because I've lived in the countryside for the last twenty-four years (and also for my first six years), I've absorbed this North American Great Plains landscape into my blood and bones, and I know things about it now that makes me intensely admiring of what I've come to understand about the system of thought of Plains Amerindian people. But I can't—I don't wish—to shake off my absorption in European culture. It's a dilemma I'm not the first Western North American writer to point out. It's clear to me, though, that our "two solitudes" have to come to some kind of an accord, some kind of livable recognition of each other's rights and wisdom.

I have begun to have an idea of the continents of the world—I've been only in North America, Europe, and, briefly, Africa—as each being a complete, self-enclosing, and unique world. By this I mean not just the climatic systems or the geographical or the biological worlds, but especially the world of the spiritual. I remember thinking when I was in Africa in 1995 that I understood why the colonizers referred to Africa by the now-hated phrase, "the dark continent," but that it had nothing to do with the skin colour of its many diverse peoples, or even of the soil, which also is greatly varied, or of the differing spiritual systems of its many cultures. It had instead to do with some indefinable richness that hovered in the air, indescribable—at least for one there hardly a month—that was an essence not to be pinpointed or amenable to scientific investigation. Even now, trying mentally to compare this *thing* I perceived faintly, on the edge of my awareness when I was there, to the aura or ambience of this continent I know so well, I feel a great difference, not an aura I can easily describe, though, but of equal beauty and power.

To carry this idea through logically, I try to think of what I felt when travelling in Europe and I get no sense at all of an *essence*, as if that continent is far too varied, its cultures so profoundly involved in art and literature and treasures of history—unless that is its essence—that sniffing the air for a measure of its true nature, I come away with nothing.

Surprised in Addis Ababa to see stunted goats and cattle wandering in and out of the thick stream of traffic on the main thoroughfare of this city of then three million, I asked an African with us, who lived in South Africa, if this was typical of African cities. He glanced around, then said, "Yes, in the sense of the closeness to nature." No one would ever say that of European cities, and North America, I think, occupies a middle position in this scale.

Every continent has evolved its own variety of spiritual life, eroded to varying degrees by the advent of missionaries and travellers from elsewhere bringing the ideas of their own continents to places where they may very well not fit at all. Or it may be not that the variety of spiritual life evolved but, as I see it, that it was a *given*, along with the varieties of trees and soil and insects and animals, and each set of indigenous peoples slowly discovered it or grew up with it as it grew up.

Vine Deloria, Jr., an influential Lakota writer and historian, says, in *God Is Red*, that this was a new continent; a new continent needs new understanding, that is, new gods, new systems of spirituality, that Christianity might have worked in Europe, but it did not—does not—work for this continent. (Surely the ongoing destruction of Nature is evidence of this.)

Further, the Amerindian people already had the system that belonged to—that fitted, that came out of—this continent, if only Europeans had listened to them. I think that the Amerindians arrived at their beliefs and the accompanying rituals through their attentiveness to and their compliance with the land. For this bond, there is, there can be, no substitute.

This, I think, with all its implications, is finally what we stole from Amerindian people when we stole their land. Because we did not believe what they told us about their understanding of the natural world, and because we stole their children so that they would never again be able fully to believe what their old people told them about the world, and no longer knew who they were, we came near to destroying them, too.

The famous case of the Gitskan and Wet'suwet'en fighting for their hereditary lands in British Columbia must surely have helped more people to understand the Amerindian point of view. The hereditary chiefs, Gisday Wa and Delgam Uukw, presented their case to the Supreme Court in a written (and later published) brief called *In the Spirit of the Land: Statement of the Gitskan and Wet'-suwet'en Hereditary Chiefs in the Supreme Court of British Columbia, 1987–1990*:

For us, the ownership of territory is a marriage of the Chief and the land. Each Chief had an ancestor who encountered and acknowledged the life of the land. From such encounters come power. The land, the plants, the animals and the people all have spirit—they all must be shown respect. That is the basis of our law.... When the chief directs his house properly and the laws are followed, then that original power can be recreated.

My power [Delgam Uukw] is carried in my House's histories, songs, dances and crests. It is recreated at the Feast when the histories are told, songs and dances performed and crests displayed. With the wealth that comes from respectful use of the territory, the House feeds the name of the Chief in the Feast Hall. In this way, the law, the Chief, the territory and the Feast become one.

The Gitskan and Wet'suwet'en speak of "the life of the land," and reiterate, as so do many Amerindian societies, that the land, the plants, the animals, and the people have spirit and must be shown respect.

Take away the land from people who are a part of the land and not only do you take away their ability to support themselves, you take away their spiritual base, for without the land all else in the culture loses its basis, its sense, its natural rhythms, its coherence, its entire life-giving and spirit-nourishing *raison d'être*. Not to mention the damage done to a people from centuries-old mourning and grief, from endless poverty, from constant, endemic injustice, humiliations, and disenfranchisement of nearly every kind. Take away land from *us* and we may be impoverished, but we still have our schools, churches, governments, and hierarchy of relationships. We may lose status, but our belief systems, which create our culture and sustain us within it, remain intact.

One day, walking in the field, I crossed a hill I had often crossed and noticed for the first time that I could remember, although how I could have missed it I don't know, that on this one low hill there were—I counted them in disbelief and some rising emotion that took me by surprise—four burial cairns. How great the deaths must have been here, I thought, and spontaneous tears of grief and shock at so many deaths sprang to my eyes.

All those years I'd walked that field and seen the cairns, and not seen them, and then rediscovered them, and lost them again, only to see them once more, and I had felt no emotion other than surprise and sometimes pleasure at finding them, as if I were particularly perspicacious and vigilant and deserving.

Now what I felt was what I should have felt all along, if I had believed the bones of those beneath the cairns were once living and walking and breathing human beings: that they were *people. People* had died here, and those who loved them had buried them in sorrow. I wept for a moment, and my grieving was for once genuine. I felt ashamed that I had not felt this before, that I'd been so proud of myself, so possessive of what was not mine at all, of a place where I walked only on the sufferance of the ancestral spirits guarding it, and only because those to whom this field and those graves rightly belonged had been rendered powerless to stop me.

The eminent American writer Gary Snyder, in *The Practice of the Wild*, in an essay called "The Place, the Region, and the Commons," says this:

Sometime in the mid-seventies at a conference of Native American leaders and activists in Bozeman, Montana, I heard a Crow elder say something similar: "You know, I think if people stay somewhere long enough—even white people—the spirits will begin to speak to them. It's the power of the spirits coming up from the land. The spirits and the old powers aren't lost, they just need people to be around long enough and the spirits will begin to influence them."

To understand the profound meaning of land—to walk on it with the respect, born of real understanding, of the traditional Amerindian, to see it as sacred—is to be terrified, shattered, humbled, and, in the end, joyous. It is to come home at last.

Epilogue

THE GIFT

MY UNNATURAL AND INEXPLICABLE TIREDNESS HAD LEFT
me. It began to leave when I began to write this book. I was deeply
grateful to have it gone, and smug in a mildly rueful way that it had
left as mysteriously as it had come, proving, I thought, that its
source hadn't been anything a doctor could cure. I'd been right in
my suspicion that it had something to do with the field.

The haunting of our house had mostly died down too. It had
been years since we'd heard footsteps coming up the hall as we lay
rigid in bed, listening, years since the doorknob had turned without
the door opening, or coins had rattled on the dresser. We still woke
sometimes and remarked to each other, "The house was noisy last
night," and that was all. I noticed now that this noisiness was sometimes connected to the deaths of people we knew. More often we
didn't know the reason, but the haunting, a pale shadow of what it
had once been, no longer frightened or even disturbed us. It, too,
had been connected to the field, we felt, and having discovered the
true nature of the field, we no longer needed disturbing, shaking up,
some sense knocked into our thick heads.

And now the field had sound. I remembered how, when I first

began to go there, I was struck by how silent it was, not a bird, not an insect, except for the occasional creepily silent wood tick. Now when I entered the field, went to the centre and stood there quietly, I was surrounded by a symphony of whistles, chirps, cheeps, trills, hums, buzzes, clicks, whirrs, rattles, hoots, and the occasional shriek of a hawk. Now if I paid attention, I saw horned larks, meadowlarks, killdeers, lark buntings, and a number of other birds to which I never got close enough to name if I'd wanted to. I saw the native grasshoppers that had always been there, and the black beetles and the mosquitoes, but now there were also blue dragonflies, huge black-and-yellow or orange bees, and several different kinds and colours of butterflies.

After thirteen years without cattle in the field, abundance in the form of plant life had returned as well. In places the wild grasses were knee-high, and everywhere I looked, there were big patches of Indian breadroot, and wildflowers of such numbers and variety that would take your breath away. Even the hardpan was shrinking in size, small clusters of grass taking root on its borders and growing singly here and there in its centre. The juniper was lush and green on all the hillsides and scented the air with its perfume. A hundred and one plants I couldn't name bloomed and flowered and swayed and whispered in the breeze. I had never seen such beauty.

There had always been animal trails in the field, but now there were more than twice as many. Where once animals could hide only by going down a burrow or running behind a hill or a rock, the grass on each side of their trails would now hide them. Now there were a few gophers standing bright-eyed and upright as posts at the entrance to their narrow burrows. Even the jackrabbits had returned to their natural habitat, just a few, but big as small dogs, able to bound a huge distance in one leap if so inclined. Now that I'd seen one very big snake which I'd taken to be a bull or gopher snake, although I had then and still do have some doubts about this, I had an idea where to look for them and investigated, and there was another, this one so perfect an example of a bull snake as to have come alive from a biology textbook. And on another day, when I was not even snake-hunting, a snake tore past my feet so quickly I saw only his nether half as it disappeared down a hole, and a grey-green all-over pattern which I could describe only as "sort of tweedy." It wasn't a bull snake, a rattlesnake, or a garter snake. Were there once so many snakes on the prairie? I wondered.

I had some sense that my time with the field, this exploration, this discovery, was coming to an end. Or, if not an end, to some culmination of experience I could not identify in advance or guess at. I only knew that, as the field was a sacred place and one full of graves of the true owners of this land, I could not have it all to myself forever, that all of this discovery was leading somewhere even if I couldn't guess where.

Well, I had my book to write, I thought, about all the things I'd learned from my devotion to the field, what it had taught me, and why what it had taught me mattered. I couldn't imagine, though, that the day would come when I could walk away from the field and not look back with a broken heart.

But somehow I knew that that day was coming, I felt it in my heart or hovering in the air around me; it would come, one way or another, and I had better act as if it were, as if I knew what the appropriate thing to do was. I didn't know, but suddenly it seemed right to me that I should set myself to the task I'd promised myself to do and never had: a mapping of the field, of each cairn and stone circle and pile of rocks. I knew now that I'd never do it properly, hadn't the patience, no longer felt the need for an exact mapping, if I'd even had the skill and knowledge to do it. So instead, in some perplexing but firm motivation to get it done, I set out to walk the field from north to south, in sections, one by one, moving from east to west. I carried a small notebook in my pocket only three inches by five inches, and a ballpoint pen, and I made rough sketches of what I found as I went.

I developed a system: *pc* meant "possible cairn"; a filled-in circle meant that here was definitely a cairn; a circle with the letter *c* inside it meant a stone circle; a few scribbled small circles meant that I had no idea what this was, but it looked as if it might once have been something. It took me a month and filled most of my little notebook with diagrams and notations which once done I could hardly make sense of.

But once done, I never did count up all the *pc*s or the certain cairns or the definite circles. Long before I finished my walk of every square inch of the field (as I liked to tell myself), uphill and down, I saw the futility of trying to do so. But I kept on anyway, doggedly, for two reasons: first, because I said to myself that this was worth doing since I was bearing witness to the dead of this field, every one of them, and to the evidences of a people driven out of their homeland, forbidden even to enter it any more. I would be a witness to the field.

Second, because the more I walked, step by step, past and sometimes into cactus, and around badger, gopher, snake, mice, and insect holes, and around rocks and greasewood shrubs, trying not to step on plants—impossible task—I was finding things I hadn't seen before. Or perhaps I had, but not in this new way; I had new eyes now, I told myself, but often I was so surprised by what I was seeing, or had seen before and forgotten and not seen again and now was seeing in a new way, that I thought the field (how else to conceptualize this *presence*) was showing me what it wanted me at last to know.

Now the cairns stood up for me and declared themselves, and I was sure they'd never risen so high above the level before. I walked systematically, and things I'd passed by on other days, intent on other things, I now *saw*. I found a large solidly black rock, and I thought that just maybe I'd found flint, a perfect source for tools and weapons. The tops and sides looked to me as if just maybe humans and not glaciers had broken off the pieces that had clearly been broken away. Then I noticed there seemed to be a stone path leading on an angle away from the rock thirty or more feet to a stone pile. I had no idea what that meant, if anything. I scribbled notes and drawings in an unreadable hand on my tiny pages and moved on to my next section.

I found a petroglyph. Or I thought it was one. I was walking with Peter and there it was, hidden in an out-of-the-way spot, and I called him over, so excited I could hardly speak. We stared at it, and now neither of us knew if it was done by human hands or by thousands of years of erosion, which could produce almost any shape. The rock was granite, pink granite, and I knew most petroglyphs in this part of the West were done in softer rock, and they were in prominent places, not out of sight like this one. And the markings themselves were not renderings of animals or people as they usually are, but ridges in the stone. I was reminded of ribstones, although this wasn't much like a ribstone, either. (Ribstones are humped rocks whose backs and sides have "ribs" carved in them with a perpendicular line down the rock's centre from which the "ribs" emanate.) Still, we didn't believe these marks could have been done by a glacier, and as I kept saying, "I've walked this field from top to bottom and one end to the other, and there is not another stone like it in the field."

I wasn't absolutely convinced myself, though, and so on the summer solstice I went to the field about nine in the morning (at sunrise there had been cloud), straight to my petroglyph, and looked at it. I came away convinced it was indeed done by human hands. This was incredibly exciting. To think all the years this field had been a part of our lives and we'd never known there was an actual petroglyph there. Peter, however, remained dubious.

We called an archeologist, part of whose mandate it is to evaluate such sites. Only two weeks passed and she arrived, bringing with her two Amerindian men, one an elder, the other a young man working in the heritage field for his people. I had waited in a state of great tension all morning and struggled to hide my excitement at their arrival. I had no idea what would happen next, but out to the field we went, the three of them and Peter and me.

We went first to the "petroglyph." The men studied it, but did not comment; the archeologist was kind and not final, but she didn't believe the marks on the rock were done by human hands. The cairns were real; "A lot of people were buried here," one of the men said. The possible vision-quest site was actually a grave; about this they said there was no doubt. The elder walked the field alone, often far from the rest of us, squatting sometimes, in silence, looking at the ground or holding a stone in his hand, perhaps listening, or listening to an inner voice only he could hear. He said little. The younger man said of him, softly, "Stones talk to him."

I showed them the boulder of black stone on the high cliff and the strange line of stones leading away from it for thirty or more feet. The large black rock they identified as "probably basalt"—I'd been hoping it was flint. At once they remarked that the line of stones looked like a "bison-drive line," that is, an arrangement of stones designed to guide a herd in the direction hunters wanted them to go, in this case, over a buffalo jump. Only a few days before, some-one had picked up a fossilized bone fragment from the area below this, and Tim Tokaryk had said it just might be from a buffalo. Maybe under the soil and stone I'd so often walked over, there lay a vast cache of buffalo bones.

The plateau that held the stone circle—perhaps from the remains of a Blackfoot burial tent, I thought they identified at once as an effigy of a turtle. That it was an effigy accounted for the stone path-way up to it, and also, although I never mentioned this to them, the fact that this hill was the first and last in the field lit by the rising and setting sun each day. The possiblity of this circle being an effigy had never entered my head, and made up for their—at least the archeol-ogist's—disbelief about the petroglyph. I say "the archeologist's disbelief" because the two Amerindian men didn't say what they thought of it.

I tried to tell a little about the things I had observed or under-stood that were not strictly factual, not part of the physical field. The elder walked away; the younger man disagreed and provided differ-ent explanations. I told a very brief version of the visit of the Amerindian woman from the West Coast, and I felt their disbelief, or at least that of one of them, although neither said anything. But, I thought, they hadn't heard that wild, haunted cry from deep in these hills when she'd addressed the field in her own language.

Both were courteous, soft-spoken, gentle in their demeanour, gravely hiding their thoughts, or so I thought. We told them that we'd protect the field, not let anyone else in, not even allow cattle to graze in it, that any of their people who wanted to come to it for ceremonies were welcome. We would keep it safe for them, and for no other purpose. They did not say what they knew or what they thought; I knew that almost certainly we would never know. They would never tell us.

Their visit was so disturbing to me that when they left, I felt as though I were suspended in a huge, dark cavern and I couldn't rest or find respite or solid footing. I didn't know what to think and I wondered if I was mad, had been subjected to madness. I thought of all the things I didn't say to them, the stories I didn't tell them about what had happened to me in the field, and was glad I hadn't. Time passed, and I began to find my footing again. I am not an Amerindian woman, I am a daughter of the oppressors, I reminded myself. There are things I have no right to know; they have no obligation to tell me anything.

A day passed, and then another, and I did not even look out at the field. On the next when I woke, the sun was shining, the leaves on the poplars outside the kitchen windows glistened as they turned in the light breeze and the sunshine. It had been so far a sunless summer, mornings like this one were precious, and although I didn't think I'd ever go to the field again, it came gradually to me that this was the day I would return and see what was left of my long association with it. I'd see what would happen now when I was there. And I felt happy, no reason for it, just happy, and surprisingly I approached the field without trepidation, but with pleasure—I was even humming to myself.

It had never been more beautiful; I thought that heaven itself could not be more beautiful, more peaceful, more constantly interesting, more whole and complete and yet mysterious. I began to walk aimlessly, and I found that I wanted to return once more to the petroglyph. When I reached it, I stared at it, wondering, and then sat on the ground below it. A great sadness entered my heart,

The Gift

I found I'd begun silently, in my puzzling misery, to cry.

What do you want of the field? that "voiceless voice," after years of silence, now asked in my head. It still had the capacity to get right to the heart of the matter, and I knew this was the crucial question. Things here in the field seemed to have come to an end for me, and how was I to absorb this? What was I to do now?

I was bewildered, because I no longer knew the answer, I was floundering, full of loss. What could I want of it? To begin over again, retrace my steps until I reached this day again? To stumble over some new, engrossing mystery? Did I want to be desperately unhappy again and full of questions about the meaning of life so that I had to use the field to calm and comfort me? Not that, I thought, and I remembered, *This, too, is illusion.* I got up and wandered away to the nearest pile of stones, the one that just might be another grave. I walked around it and thought. Truly, what did I want of it now?

I thought of all the field had taught me, most of it recorded in this book; how most of it no one would believe, or they would classify me as crazy or a liar or both. Did I have the courage to go ahead with the writing, or would it be real madness to do so? I thought of how, for safety's sake, to end my book I might say that I had written a myth, although every word of it was true, as all myths are true. A lovely dodge, of course, one that would save my reputation and would at the same time glorify mystery.

I found I didn't want to say that. I resisted it, because it seemed to me a lie, and I wouldn't end such hard-won truth with a lie, even one that I knew readers would find easier to believe than the truth and that critics would find more enchantingly literary than the less beautiful truth. I found now that I could only say that *I knew what I knew* and that the great lesson of my nearly sixty years has been that no matter what the price, I would no longer refuse or deny my own experience.

All of this—this probably-not-a-petroglyph, these burial cairns, these stone circles with their ceremonial piles of stones, this possible turtle effigy, these artifacts I'd found and lost, and found again, even the event I treasured most, the small, glistening Indian breadroot plant appearing on the path before me—seemed less important now that Peter and I had given it all back, at least in spirit, if not in outright ownership yet, to the people to whom it belonged. Whatever it was the field had meant to me I felt shifting and changing now.

I walked a little more, and thought. All around us the farming economy on which we and our friends and neighbours have depended since our families' arrival as settlers from Europe a hundred years ago is in shambles. Every day brings more bad news. Everyone, us included, recognizes that we can no longer afford to farm or ranch, that with every passing year in economic terms we go farther backward. The great dream of the settlers, mostly poor people, seems to be ending as, once again, a handful of entrepreneurs begin to take over most of the land.

I remembered the last stand of the Great Plains people of this area—to have all of southwest Saskatchewan as their homeland in the form of contiguous reserves—a dream that was refused out of hand. I thought of how the Nekaneet people are buying back their own land, how even the Carry the Kettle people have begun their return to the Cypress Hills, and I wondered if perhaps in the second millennium it will be fulfilled. I even hoped it would happen, slowly, as we occupiers die off, sell out, are bankrupted, and one way or another leave.

Gazing up the cliffsides and down the grassy bowl behind me, I thought of how I'd taken people to the field for a pleasing ramble before or after dinner and said nothing about what I knew was there, and how they walked past burial cairns and stone circles and never even saw them, as if they weren't there at all, although I could see them plainly. I thought of how even I myself had walked there for years and had seen nothing until one day, somehow, I'd begun to see.

How strange it was that the settlers, my own people on both sides, too, could not *see* what was there all over the prairie. They'd used the stones to build dams and for foundations for their buildings, they'd picked them so they could farm—"The circles always went first," Peter said, "because they were so easy to see."—and yet, even knowing what they were doing, they didn't *see*. Beyond seeing, there was *recognizing*. I couldn't find a better word for what I meant; that a lot of people had lived here for a very long time, that they were not "picking rock" so they could farm, that they were dismantling the remains of a civilization. Every stone freighted with tears, with the weight of grief, they should have been too heavy to lift.

If the settlers had seen, recognized, admitted that actuality, instead of blinding themselves to it, none of the rest of the horror would have happened, because even though they were merely pawns in a much bigger game, and struggling with their own human needs, they would not have been able to be a part of what was, in the end, evil.

"This was all prophesied, you know," the young Amerindian visitor had said that afternoon to us. "It was prophesied that it would get very bad before it began to get better." Peter said, "Is it getting better?" and he nodded yes, mutely. I hoped very much that he meant that Peter and I were part of the "getting better" and not of the "getting worse."

What did I want of the field now? The peace, the great beauty, the profound sense of connectedness with some unseen power—the mysterious "voiceless voice," the wind blowing through the tall grass and whispering, a torrent of voices speaking words to me that I couldn't understand, that made me shake my head in a frantic passion of desire and sorrow. Yes, all of that.

My odyssey is ended, I thought. For twenty years or more this field, the nature in it, the birds, the animals, the plants, the history, the voices from all the long past of this stony planet, have spoken to me and taught me and held out promise to me of answers to the great questions: Who are we? From where have we come? Where are we going? Why? It is as if I've been taken to the very brink where the answers lie, as far as one can go, to the distant edge of this physical world, and allowed a glimpse through the veil into another one.

I knew my knowledge of the field was a gift given me, but it was not just for me. Surely it was given me only so that I might pass it on to others, in the same way as we had begun to do with the field and the Amerindian people. I would try to give it to those most needing to know these teachings, those who saw without seeing, who knew and denied what they knew. I would try to transform the gift given me by the field into a payment and a tribute to ease the wild stone heart of the earth.

AUTHOR'S NOTE

THE READER WILL NOTICE THE OCCASIONAL ANNOYING
vagueness about detail: the location of the field, the description of
the "petroglyph," the identity of certain people. I apologize, but
find these necessary so as not to offend others, or to make vulnerable the sacred or the precious. I have chosen to use the term
"Amerindians," used by Dr. Olive Dickason, who wrote *Canada's
First Nations: A History of Founding Peoples From Earliest Times*, to
refer to the people we grew up calling—inaccurately and often, if
not usually, offensively—"Indians."

I owe thanks to more people than I am able to name or who
would wish to be named, especially to my Haisla friend, Louise
Barbetti. However, archeologists Dr. David Meyer of the University of Saskatchewan and Dr. Margaret Hanna of the Royal
Saskatchewan Museum were always ready to answer my questions,
as was Dr. Donald Mitchell, also an archeologist and professor
emeritus, University of Victoria. All of them walked the field with
me. Tim Tokaryk, manager of the Eastend Fossil Research Station,
also gave me papers, explained matters that baffled me, gave me the
names of things I'd never have found for myself. Greg Grace led me

to a deeper understanding of the fascination of dinosaurs, and Robert Gebhardt lent me books on rocks. Zoheir Abouguendia, Jeff Thorpe, and Bob Godwin, experts all, with unflappable good nature answered my questions about plants. Linda Smith Stowell, Unitarian minister, took the time to discuss her doctoral thesis with me. They are all part of the story, as are those unnamed but much appreciated friends, guests, visitors, and officials who stopped by, tramped the field with us, and talked to us about what they knew. As always, Peter supported and helped me, Jan Whitford encouraged me, and Phyllis Bruce's remarkable editorial skills kept me on track. I couldn't have written this book without them.

SOURCES

GENERAL READING

Cirlot, J. E. *A Dictionary of Symbols*. London: Routledge and Kegan Paul, 1962.

Cook-Lynn, Elizabeth. *Why I Can't Read Wallace Stegner and Other Essays: A Tribal Voice*. Madison: University of Wisconsin Press, 1996.

Culhane, Dara. *The Pleasure of the Crown: Anthropology, Law and First Nations*. Burnaby, B.C.: Talonbooks, 1998.

Deloria, Vine, Jr. *God Is Red*. New York: Grosset and Dunlap, 1973.

DiSilvestro, Roger. *Reclaiming the Last Wild Places: A New Agenda for Biodiversity*. New York: John Wiley and Sons, 1993.

Estés, Clarissa Pinkola. *Women Who Run With the Wolves: Myths and Stories of the Wild Woman Archetype*. New York: Ballantine Books, 1992.

Fernandez-Armesto, Felipe. *Truth: A History and a Guide for the Perplexed*. London: A Black Swan Book, 1998.

Frazer, James G. *The Golden Bough: The Roots of Religion and Folklore*. London: Macmillan, 1890; New York: Crown Publishers, 1981.

Hoxie, Frederick, ed. *Encyclopedia of North American Indians*. Boston: Houghton Mifflin, 1996.

Hunter, Robert, and Robert Calihoo. *Occupied Canada: A Young White Man Discovers His Unsuspected Past*. Toronto: McClelland & Stewart, 1991.

Irwin, Lee. *The Dream Seekers: Native American Visionary Traditions of the Great Plains*. Norman: University of Oklahoma Press, 1994.

Jung, Carl. *Memories, Dreams, Reflections*. New York: Random House, 1961.

Kehoe, Thomas F. *Stone Tipi Rings in North-Central Montana and the Adjacent Portion of Alberta, Canada: Their Historical, Ethnological, and Archeological Aspects*. Smithsonian Institution, Bureau of American Ethnology, Bulletin 173. Undated.

Lévi-Strauss, Claude. *The Savage Mind*. Chicago: University of Chicago Press, 1962, 1966.

Mails, Thomas E. *Fools Crow*. Lincoln: University of Nebraska Press, 1979.

McClintock, Walter. *The Old North Trail or Life, Legends and Religion of the Blackfeet Indians*. London: Macmillan and Co., 1910.

McLuhan, T. C. *The Way of the Earth: Encounters With Nature in Ancient and Contemporary Thought*. New York: Touchstone, Simon & Schuster, 1994.

McLuhan, T. C. *Touch the Earth*. New York: Outerbridge and Dienstfry, 1971; New York: Simon & Schuster, 1992.

Pyle, Robert. *Where Bigfoot Walks: Crossing the Great Divide*. Boston: Houghton Mifflin, 1995.

Ross, Rupert. *Dancing With a Ghost: Exploring Indian Reality*. Toronto: Reed Books Canada, Distributed by McClelland & Stewart, 1992.

Schama, Simon. *Landscape and Memory*. Toronto: Random House, 1995.

Smith Stowell, Linda. "Subjective Religious Experience Among Unitarian

Universalists: A Generational Study." Unpublished thesis in partial fulfilment of the requirements for the degree Doctor of Ministry, School of Theology, Claremont, 1995.

Snyder, Gary. *The Practice of the Wild*. San Francisco: North Point Press, 1990.

St. Pierre, Mark, and Tilda Long Soldier. *Walking in the Sacred Manner*. New York: A Touchstone Book, Simon & Schuster, 1995.

Stegner, Wallace. *Wolf Willow: A History, a Story, and a Memory of the Last Plains Frontier*. New York: The Viking Press, 1955, 1962.

Stonechild, Blair, and Bill Waiser. *Loyal Till Death: Indians and the North-West Rebellion*. Calgary: Fifth House, 1997.

Storer, John. *Geological History of Saskatchewan*. Regina: Saskatchewan Museum of Natural History, 1989.

Wa, Gisday, and Delgam Uukw. *In the Spirit of the Land: Statement of the Gitksan and Wet'suwet'en Hereditary Chiefs in the Supreme Court of British Columbia, 1987–1990*, Gabriola, B.: Reflections, 1989, 1992.

Underhill, Evelyn. *Mysticism: A Study in the Nature and Development of Man's Spiritual Consciousness*. New York: New American Library, 1974.

BOOKS ABOUT PLANTS AND THEIR USES

Budd, A. C. *Budd's Flora of the Canadian Prairie Provinces*. Rev. and enlarged by Looman and Best. Research Branch, Agriculture Canada, 1979.

Johnson, Hope. *Prairie Plants of Southeast Alberta*. Medicine Hat: Southeast Alberta Regional Planning Commission, 1983, 1984.

Kindscher, Kelly. *Medicinal Wild Plants of the Prairie: An Enthnobotanical Guide*. Lawrence, Kansas: University Press of Kansas, 1992.

Looman, J. *III Range and Forage Plants of the Canadian Prairies*. Research Branch, Agriculture Canada, 1983.

Peacock, Sandra Leslie. "Piikani Ethnobotany: Traditional Plant Knowledge of the Piikani Peoples of the Northwestern Plains." Master's thesis, University of Calgary, 1992.

Root Woman and Dave. *Native Medicines*. Saskatchewan: Root Woman and Dave, 1994.

The Root Woman—Kahlee Keane. *Useful Wild Plants of Saskatchewan: Book 1*. Saskatchewan: Root Woman and Dave, 1992, 1994.

———. *More Useful Wild Plants of Saskatchewan: Book 2*. Saskatchewan: Root Woman and Dave, 1994.

Vance, F. R., J. R. Jowsey and J. S. McLean. *Wildflowers Across the Prairies*. Saskatoon: Western Producer Prairie Books, 1984, 1986.

Vitt, Dale H., Janet E. Marsh and Robin B. Bovey. *Mosses, Lichens and Ferns of Northwest North America*. Edmonton: Lone Pine Publishing, 1988.

Blackfoot Camp

all dry & covered
...o.

July 18, 1859

Crossing Pl 35 yds

Red Deer R.

Valley 250 ft deep

Sandy Waste

Boulders

Sands Waste

Some large Poplar trees on the
River points. Abundance of
Game; Great profusion of
boulders.

Salt Pools

Very Arid

N   S

Hilly
&
Arid

Very Hilly
no good pasture

Rattlesnake
Camp

Bluff of Poplar

Crossing Pl. 250 yds.

Val. very deep

L. Blood Ind.

Some good pasture
no timber

Sand hill Cr.

Blood Ind⁵

Range of Hills continue to the

the Cyprés Hills

South Saskatchewan R.

... ft deep

On the low level pasture bad

Pasture pretty good
no timber & little
water.

... 300 yds. wide

... 700   "

Camp July

Maple Cr.

Marine Tertiary Fossils

Coulée

Swamp

Arid rolling prairie
traversed by Coulées

...ings

L. Peehopee
(Pakekeo of
U.S. Survey)

Terrace
of Shingle

...Coulée

...r pasture

Cyprés Hills
8800 feet.

Rich Pasture in the hollows
& very hilly.

Valley well timbered with Pines, Spruce
Maple, &c.   Camp, Aug. 1859.

Great abundance of game & Wild
fruit in the valleys.

1600 ft above the Plain.

Base of Cyprés Hills & of Watershed
of Missouri, 3261 ft above the Sea.

To the Missouri

Mr Sullivan, Augt 1859

Val. 200
...sh pools
...gs.

Milk   River

Three Buttes

D

111°   110°   109°